CW00687106

A FLORILEGIUM

Sheffield's Hidden Garden

Arum italicum 'Marmoratum'. Artist: Rosalind Timperley
Graphite pencil and watercolour. Accepted to the Archive 2013.

A FLORILEGIUM
Sheffield's Hidden Garden

VALERIE OXLEY

THE CROWOOD PRESS

First published in 2021 by
The Crowood Press Ltd
Ramsbury, Marlborough
Wiltshire SN8 2HR

enquiries@crowood.com
www.crowood.com

British Library Cataloguing-in-Publication Data
A catalogue record for this book is available from the British Library.

ISBN 978 1 78500 894 8

Cover design: Peggy & Co. Design
Pen and ink logo design: Jenny Kirkland
Crinodendron hookerianum Elaine Shimwell. Coloured pencil. Accepted to the Archive 2004

Dedication
This book is dedicated to the members, past and present, of The Florilegium Society at Sheffield Botanical Gardens, whose enthusiasm and generosity have enabled the Society to compile an important archive of drawings and paintings of the planting at the Gardens for everyone to enjoy.

Typeset and designed by Peggy & Co. Design
Printed and bound in India by Parksons Graphics

Lathraea clandestina Anne Dent. Graphite pencil and watercolour. Accepted to the Archive 2003

Contents

Rosa moyesii Arnolda Beynon. Graphite pencil and watercolour.
Accepted to the Archive 2003

Preface

The Botanical Gardens in Sheffield are a much-loved public space. Just sitting quietly on a sunny day one can observe how people use and enjoy the Gardens, each in their own unique way. Some simply use the Gardens to get from A to B: a conduit from a busy shopping area to a quiet residential one. Some people walk briskly through, rucksacks hauled onto their backs, hurrying to school or to attend a lecture at the University. Others, mums or dads, walk at a more leisurely pace with young children in tow, going to meet other young parents at the café or to sit on the grass whilst the children play. Then there are the school visits; eager young children, chattering happily, skipping and dancing through the gardens with their teachers. Older children arrive, questionnaires in hand, looking for a particular tree or herbaceous plant to make a sketch or answer a question. These visitors are followed by those who simply come because they love the place and always have done.

But this is more than a pleasure garden full of beautiful trees and colourful plants; it is a collection of gardens where one can study plants from all round the world. There are amazing plants, some originating from rainforests where their existence is threatened, plants that in the wild would be found clinging to a mountain side or at the bottom of a deep ravine. Plants that are especially adapted to grow in arid areas and those that have been saved from extinction. Plants that grow in the restored pavilions, a special place, where they are protected from the rigours of the winter months. Each plant is unique and each one has a story to tell.

It was not difficult to persuade local botanical artists that on their doorstep was a wonderful resource for botanical art: a whole garden full of interesting and unusual plants just waiting for their portraits to be painted, and for their botanical secrets and histories to be written.

The naming of plants is constantly changing: scientists argue about taxonomy and DNA has played its part in adding to the confusion, so it is a struggle to keep up. Scientific names are either unknown, misunderstood or difficult to pronounce; we have become disconnected and ignorant about their importance. But as you will discover when reading this book, they tell us a great deal about the plant, very often in just two words.

This book is a tribute to the artists, past and present members of The Florilegium Society, who have generously given of their time and artistic expertise to record in detail a selection of the plants at Sheffield Botanical Gardens. The artists have attempted to explain through drawing and painting how a plant works, its habit and life cycle. The plant's collecting history has been added to complete the profile.

The Committee and members of The Florilegium Society hope you will enjoy your journey through this florilegium. Please take time to linger by the plants and discover, as we have done, the secrets of Sheffield's 'Hidden Garden'.

Helleborus x *hybridus* Jill Holcombe. Graphite pencil and watercolour. Accepted to the Archive 2005

Foreword

In July 2001 Dr James Joseph White, who was Curator of Art and Principal Research Scholar at the Hunt Institute for Botanical Documentation, Carnegie Mellon University, Pittsburgh, wrote a letter enthusiastically supporting the establishment of a florilegium society at Sheffield Botanical Gardens and became one of its first Patrons. After Dr White's retirement his assistant Lugene B. Bruno became the Curator of Art. The members of The Florilegium Society at Sheffield Botanical Gardens were delighted when, after the sad death of Dr White, Lugene Bruno agreed to represent the Hunt Institute and become a Patron of the Society.

In the seventeenth century, exotic plants were arriving in Europe through correspondents and voyages of exploration. Admired for their beauty and interesting characteristics, these unusual plants were avidly collected for university botanic gardens and the pleasure gardens of wealthy owners.

Along with this abundance of exotica was a desire to document these plant collections in beautifully illustrated publications known as florilegia. The development of the printmaking processes of etching and engraving on metal plates and the embellishment of these prints with hand colouring made it possible to achieve remarkable results. A magnificent example from this period is Basilius Besler's *Hortus Eystettensis* (1613), which includes 367 engravings of plants from the Prince-Bishop of Eichstätt's garden in Germany, which are arranged by the season.

The popularity of florilegia continued through the eighteenth and nineteenth centuries, but these vied with the illustrated scientific texts, which focused on floras and monographs of specific regions and families. These publications are still relevant, not only for their beauty but because they document the history of the native and introduced species of each period.

By the late twentieth century, the importance of the history and future of this art form was recognized and culminated in exhibitions of historical and contemporary botanical art.

It is only natural that this renewal of interest in plants and gardens led to a desire to once again create florilegia that document the native and cultivated plants of a specific place or garden. The Chelsea Physic Garden Florilegium Society was the first to establish a focused group of artists in 1995, and the simultaneous interest for a group in the north of the UK was realized in 2002 as The Florilegium Society at Sheffield Botanical Gardens.

The formation of florilegium societies around the world and the relationships developed between artists, horticulturalists and botanists have bolstered the combination of aesthetically compelling and scientifically accurate representations of plants. While the florilegia of the seventeenth, eighteenth and nineteenth centuries documented the new and unusual introductions, the twenty-first-century florilegia encompass collected plants that are native, endangered, medicinal, economic and of global interest, each with an important story to tell. I applaud the dedication of these artists who have chosen to create a permanent record of our time through their extraordinary paintings and drawings.

Lugene B. Bruno,
Curator of Art and Senior Research Scholar,
Hunt Institute for Botanical Documentation

Schisandra rubriflora Judyth Pickles. Graphite pencil and watercolour. Accepted to the Archive 2013

What is a florilegium?

A florilegium, or collection of flowers, usually takes the form of an illustration accompanied by a plant profile.

The earliest collections were made for medicinal purposes and contained descriptions of plants and their medicinal properties: these books were known as herbals. The descriptions were illustrated with a drawing of the plant. Unfortunately, the plants were often copied from previous drawings without reference to the living plant and over time the plant illustrations became distorted and unrecognizable.

A step forward was made in 1542 when Leonhart Fuchs, a German physician and botanist, published a herbal in which over 490 plants were described in Latin. Fuchs was keen that the accompanying 500 woodcuts were from living specimens.

Jacques Le Moyne, a French illustrator and cartographer, worked from living plants instead of copying from previous florilegia. His work shows naturalness and attention to growth detail, such as the development of fruit and the twist and turn of leaves, that show close observation from nature.

Callistemon citrinus Cathrine Allsopp.
Graphite pencil and coloured pencil. Accepted to the Archive 2006

The early florilegia of cultivated plants contained illustrations of plants grown for interest and beauty rather than for their medicinal properties as previously. New printing methods were available and artists could choose engraving or etching as a method of reproduction.

Very often the books were divided into the four seasons, such as *Hortus Floridus*. In this florilegium the engraved copperplates were completed by Crispijn van de Passe in 1614, helped by his sons Crispijn, Simon and Willem.

Alexander Marshall, an English gardener and botanical artist, compiled a florilegium consisting of over 160 folios of plant drawings. The collection was presented to George IV in the 1820s and is the only seventeenth-century florilegium to survive to the present day.

One of the most influential artists in the history of botanical art was a Dutch painter, Gérard van Spaendonck, who was influenced by Dutch flower painters. He produced naturalistic paintings of living flowers, and contributed over fifty paintings on vellum to the collection at the Jardin du Roi in Paris between 1781 and 1785. His work was an inspiration to the artists who followed him and his reputation as a teacher was renowned. One of Spaendonck's pupils was Pierre-Joseph Redouté.

Redouté frequently drew in the Botanical Gardens in Paris. He became known to the botanist Charles Louis L'Héritier who encouraged him to follow a scientific approach and introduced him to dissection techniques. The pinnacle of his success was a flora called *Les Roses*.

Another important botanical artist was Georg Dionys Ehret, who was commissioned by a Nuremberg physician, Christoph Jacob Trew, to produce several illustrations for *Plantae Selecta* and *Hortus Nitidissimi*. During his travels Ehret met Carl Linnaeus and engraved a table for his system of classification. In his memoir Ehret wrote, 'Linnaeus explained to me his new method of examining the stamens which I could easily understand, I resolved privately to bring out a tabella of it.'

The *Banks' Florilegium* is a collection of copperplate engravings of the plants found by Joseph Banks and Daniel Solander on a voyage round the world with James Cook. The illustrator, Sydney Parkinson, did not survive the voyage and the *Florilegium* was not printed in Banks's lifetime.

Franz and Ferdinand Bauer were born in Austria and they both became meticulous botanical illustrators. Whilst Franz worked at Kew, Ferdinand accompanied Professor John Sibthorpe on a voyage to Greece, where their mission was to prepare a scientific work called *Flora Graeca*. They returned with over 1,500 sketches of flowers, animals and birds, as well as landscapes. Ferdinand prepared colour charts and numbered all parts of his sketches so the drawings could be completed after his return. Sadly, the ambitious work was not completed in the lifetime of either man and other artists finished the illustrations using Ferdinand's colour charts comprising over 1,000 colours.

Flora Londinensis was compiled by William Curtis and printed in 1777. It is a collection of plants growing wild in the London area in the mid-eighteenth century. A number of different artists prepared the copperplates, including Sydenham Edwards, James Sowerby and William Kilburn.

The Orchidaceae of Mexico and Guatemala, written by James Bateman and illustrated by Augusta Withers and Sarah Drake, is a magnificent elephant-size folio printed in 1845. It captures the obsession with orchids in the Victorian period when wealthy enthusiasts employed plant collectors to find new and rare specimens.

The Rhododendrons of the Sikkim Himalaya was compiled by Joseph Dalton Hooker with drawings and descriptions made 'on the spot'. He was the first European to collect in the Sikkim area. He suffered many setbacks and was often dispirited and weary at the end of the day. His faithful collecting companion was his dog Kinchin, who lost his whiskers in an avalanche!

A florilegium is not just a collection of meticulously drawn and painted plant illustrations: it is a lesson in history, a scientific treatise. It introduces us to a map of the world, encounters with kings and princes, intrepid plant collectors, botanists, gardeners, medics and monks!

Viburnum davidii Sheila Stancill. Graphite pencil and watercolour. Accepted to the Archive 2013

The history of the Florilegium Society at Sheffield Botanical Gardens

The idea of forming a society whose members would record the planting at Sheffield Botanical Gardens by botanical illustration was first suggested in 1995. The establishment of the Society coincided with the re-opening of the restored pavilions and the extensive restoration and replanting programme in the Gardens.

Valerie Oxley chaired a steering committee that undertook the preliminary work to set up the Society. A report was prepared for the Trustees of the Botanical Gardens asking for permission to form an independent society at the Gardens. It was envisaged that the Archive of drawings would provide a scientific and historical record of the Gardens' plants that would become a valued source of reference.

Early in the new millennium the idea became a reality, resulting in the successful launch of The Florilegium Society at Sheffield Botanical Gardens in April 2002. Supportive letters were received from the Vice-Chancellor of The University of Sheffield, Professor Robert Boucher; the Director General of the Royal Horticultural Society, Dr Andrew Colquhoun; the Director of the Royal Botanic Gardens, Kew, Professor Sir Peter Crane; and the Curator of Art and Principal Research Scholar at the Hunt Institute for Botanical Documentation, Pittsburgh, Dr James White. The supporters became the Society's first Patrons.

Professor Stephen Hopper succeeded Sir Peter Crane and agreed to become a Patron of the Society. In 2007 Judith Magee, Collections Development Manager at the Natural History Museum, London and Dr Brent Elliott, Historian to the Royal Horticultural Society, both accepted invitations to become Patrons. Lugene Bruno followed Dr White on his retirement in 2011 and agreed to become a Patron. Andrea Hart, Library Special Collections Manager at The Natural History Museum, also became a Patron in 2015 when she succeeded Judith Magee.

Dipelta floribunda Barbara Munro. Graphite pencil and watercolour. Accepted to the Archive 2016

Over the years the Society has very much appreciated the support it has received from all the Patrons and the important institutions they represent.

From the start it was agreed that anyone interested in botanical drawing could join the Society as an Associate Member. In order to become a Full Member a piece of botanical artwork had to be submitted and accepted to the Archive by a Selection Panel which would be chaired by the Society's Chairman. Other members of the panel would consist of the Curator of the Gardens, an invited botanist/horticulturalist and an artist/art historian with an interest in botanical illustration. To honour the commitment of preparing and donating work to the Archive it was decided that if a member had three artworks accepted, they would become a Fellow of the Society, an achievement to be marked by the presentation of a certificate.

In 2009 three original artworks from the Florilegium Archive were selected by Museums Sheffield for a major exhibition called 'Can Art Save Us?'. The exhibition, which explored John

Ruskin's ideas about sustainability and the environment, was funded by the Guild of St George and held at the Millennium Gallery, Sheffield. The artworks were shown alongside a florilegium from the Ruskin Collection called *Flora Londinensis* (1798).

In June 2011 the Society mounted an exhibition of archival work called 'What is a Florilegium?' at the Royal Highland Centre at Ingliston in Scotland; the display was also shown at the Royal Botanic Garden, Edinburgh for the enjoyment of the Garden's summer visitors. That same year, at The University of Sheffield, selected prints were displayed alongside florilegia from the University library's archive of books. In July 2016 the Society was invited by Lady Edward Manners to exhibit the print collection in the wonderful environment of medieval Haddon Hall in Derbyshire, and in the summer of 2017, the Society was pleased to accept another invitation to exhibit the collection when the Royal Horticultural Society held its first show in Derbyshire at Chatsworth House. In 2019 selected prints were displayed at Cusworth Hall Museum, Doncaster, alongside botanically related artefacts from the museum's collections.

The Society has a strong educational remit. The aim is to continue to help all members to develop their artistic skills through practical sessions and workshops. Understanding the botany and the naming of plants is included in the programme, with time given to the preparation of artworks for the Archive during designated painting days. A lecture programme, including nationally recognized speakers, is open to non-members.

Many members have been awarded Royal Horticultural Society medals and some have received recognition for their work worldwide. A number of members have been able to pass on their skills through teaching.

Abutilon megapotamicum Barbara Munro. Watercolour and graphite pencil. Accepted to the Archive 2009

Affiliation, in the form of friendship and mutual support, was set up with the Chelsea Physic Garden Florilegium Society in May 2001. A similar association was established with Brooklyn Botanic Garden Florilegium Society in 2003, followed in 2009 by societies at Hampton Court Palace and the Filoli Gardens, California. Affiliation was agreed with societies at the Eden Project and the Royal Botanic Garden, Sydney in 2010. The Society is proud and delighted to be part of a family of similar organizations around the world, whose common aim is to illustrate the plants growing in interesting and important gardens.

The Sheffield Botanical Gardens Trust and the Friends of the Botanical Gardens, Sheffield (FOBS) have supported the Society from the beginning. FOBS members assist by leading tours of the Gardens and help with the selection of cuttings for members to draw.

The botanical journey, learning about the plants and illustrating them for the people of Sheffield and beyond to enjoy, has been an absolute delight for all the members. Whether experienced artists or those just setting out, sharing knowledge and skills has been an important part of the Society's aims and commitment.

Valerie Oxley (Founding Chairman)
and Jill Holcombe (Founding Secretary)

The Florilegium Society's Herbarium

A herbarium is a collection of preserved plant material. Each specimen is a historical document originating from a particular time and place; the majority of specimens in university and the larger national herbaria are from plants found in the wild around the world. Many herbaria specimens are used for identification purposes and collections are being digitized to widen access. The Royal Botanic Gardens at Kew and Edinburgh and the Natural History Museum, London house important herbaria. The universities of Oxford and Cambridge have significant collections, as well as the Royal Horticultural Society at Wisley.

The Florilegium Society's Committee decided to pursue the idea of developing a herbarium to complement the Society's Archive of drawings of cultivated plants at Sheffield Botanical Gardens. It was thought a herbarium would provide additional information about the planting and become an historical record for the future.

In 2006 members of The Florilegium Society's Committee visited the Oxford University Herbaria to discover if something similar could be undertaken in Sheffield. The Herbarium Manager, Serena Marner, demonstrated different methods of preserving plant material and discussed how storage of specimens could be achieved. Serena offered to visit the Society and tutor a practical workshop for members based on the preparation of material for preservation. The proposed visit became a reality in 2007 when members were introduced to the art of preserving plant material, which involved a session stitching a pressed plant onto a sheet of thin card, using special thread and knots. This gave everyone the encouragement they needed to start planning for a herbarium to support the Archive of drawings.

In 2009 the Florilegium Society welcomed a new member, Julie Mason, who had recently completed the Society of Botanical Artists' Distance Learning Programme. Julie showed particular interest in the proposal to compile a herbarium and discussions commenced in earnest to move the project forward.

Serena Marner returned to Sheffield in 2013 to give a second workshop on preparing plant specimens, including advice on where to locate herbarium equipment. Two members, botanist Barbara Munro helped by Janice Scott, organized the purchase of materials and equipment required. This was a huge step forward; a commitment had been made. Julie started work with enthusiasm.

The majority of specimens in the Society's Herbarium are dried and pressed. Large fruits and seeds unsuitable for pressing are placed in plastic storage boxes when dried. Each plant specimen is labelled before it is placed in a press so that it is easily identified when it is removed. Once dried the plant material is stitched onto white acid-free, archival-quality herbarium sheets with white linen thread. Neutral pH adhesive is used to help attach fine petals and leaves which might otherwise become detached when handled. Papers used for drying at the pressing stage, such as blotting paper or newspaper, are changed regularly to avoid mould developing. The dried specimens are placed in a freezer for three days to ensure there are no insect infestations; this is a process which can be repeated at any time should there be concerns about pests. All the herbarium sheets are labelled with the name of the plant, the name of the collector, the date it was collected and its location in the Gardens. Important features and growth habits are also recorded on the label. The sheets are placed in folders and stored in 'Kew-style' herbarium boxes kept in an airtight cupboard.

Adiantum capillus-veneris Julie Mason. Graphite pencil and watercolour. Accepted to the Archive 2016

Herbarium specimen of *Adiantum capillus-veneris*. Prepared by Julie Mason.

The Herbarium has become an important addition to the Society's Archive of plant illustrations. In 2019 a major exhibition was held at Cusworth Hall Museum, Doncaster, where specimens from the Society's Herbarium were shown to the public for the first time, alongside matching artwork from the Society's print collection. Herbarium specimens are displayed in a similar way for members to see at the December meeting of the Society. This annual exhibition of botanical artwork from the Archive alongside a pressed specimen of the plant has become a highlight of The Florilegium Society's year and much enjoyed by members and friends.

Julie Mason (Herbarium Organizer, The Florilegium Society) with contributions from Serena Marner (Herbarium Manager, Department of Plant Sciences, University of Oxford)

The history of Sheffield Botanical Gardens 1833–2020

SHEFFIELD BOTANICAL GARDENS.

Illustration of the original conservatories by C. Gray. Robert Marnock's *Floricultural Magazine* 1836, Volume 1 Plate 2. (© With kind permission of Alison Hunter)

Sheffield is fortunate that so many of its citizens have continued to cherish these beautiful Botanical Gardens throughout their chequered history, when others, such as Leeds and Manchester, have not survived.

In 1833 a meeting was held by the wealthy townsmen of Sheffield to establish a Botanical Garden. Robert Marnock, Head Gardener at Bretton Hall, was appointed as Curator. Local architect, Benjamin Broomhead Taylor, was employed to design the buildings.

The Gardens were officially opened on 29 June 1836, an event attended by the Dukes of Norfolk and Devonshire, Earl Fitzwilliam and other notable families. Over the four opening days an estimated 12,000 people attended.

Marnock laid out the Gardens in the 'Gardenesque' style; that is, they were designed to show each plant to its advantage. He edited the *Floricultural Magazine*, which included illustrations of the plants recently discovered and introduced into the country; the local illustrators were John F. Parkin and Joshua Parkin.

Unfortunately, the late 1830s saw the final stages of a global recession that had a disastrous effect on the cutlery and steel industries in Sheffield. The management had spent over £20,000 on the Gardens and were struggling financially. The final straw was a major hailstorm in 1843, breaking some 4,770 square metres (5,700 square yards) of glass in the conservatories. The company was dissolved in February 1844 and the Gardens were put up for sale. A flurry of activity by the gentlemen of the town ensued; they sold shares for £5, thus appealing to the rising middle classes. It should be mentioned that access to the Gardens was restricted to shareholders, except on a few gala days held for the public each year. Special arrangements were made for the education of school children.

A new Botanical and Horticultural Society was created on 1 July 1844 and, with the help of a mortgage, purchased the Gardens for £9,000. John Law, from Wingerworth Hall, was appointed Curator in 1846. He published a catalogue of the collections in the Gardens in 1849, which included many of the newly introduced plants. The present Curator's House was built in 1849. Confidence grew as the debts were paid off and money became available for expansion.

Paxton successfully raised the giant water lily, *Victoria regia* (*V. amazonica*), at Chatsworth in 1849 and provided the Sheffield Gardens with seeds. Law managed to get the plants to flower in 1851. The following year a new 'Victoria House' was constructed at the western end of the conservatories around a tank 27.4 metres (30 feet) in diameter to house the lily. A matching Camellia House was erected at the eastern end in 1855. Refreshments were served in a tea pavilion, built in 1854 and described as a 'miniature Crystal Palace'; the steps for this building can still be seen in the Mediterranean Garden.

The three remaining domes (pavilions). Postcard of Edwardian painting by Warren Williams (1863–1941). (© With kind permission of Alison Hunter)

The restored pavilions. (© Photo with kind permission of Alison Hunter)

In 1858, John Ewing, gardener at Osberton Hall, was elected Curator. He served the Gardens for thirty years and was well-respected internationally for his horticultural expertise. In 1891, the Committee appointed William Harrow, who had trained at Kew and was in charge of the Cambridge Botanic Gardens, to the prestigious position of Curator.

By 1897 the Society found itself in financial difficulty again and the Committee decided to sell the Gardens. Following a public appeal, the Sheffield Town Trust, led by Sir Frederick Thorpe Mappin, agreed to buy the Gardens in 1898. New bye-laws were drawn up and the Gardens were opened free of charge to all.

In 1929, the Trust set up a separate Gardens Committee led by Sir Samuel Osborn. Osborn and his brothers donated Osborn's Field in 1934. A colonnade was built between the east and central domes in 1937, but further plans were abandoned with the start of World War II. The final piece of land added to the Gardens was donated by Osborn in 1944, and this is now the Robert Marnock Garden.

The dire state of the Gardens after the war years was a source of great concern to the Town Trust. They decided to offer them to the City Council for a 'peppercorn' rent and in 1951 the offer was accepted.

In 1984, a support group known as the Friends of the Botanical Gardens, Sheffield, was formed. Their first project was to redesign the Robert Marnock Garden. By the early 1990s the Gardens were in a desperate state. In 1994 the Council decreed that the public could work in its open spaces and the Friends' volunteers began to assist with garden maintenance and plant production. Even with the help of volunteers, the few remaining staff were unable to maintain the Gardens and the almost derelict pavilions had to be closed.

In 1996 the launch of the Urban Parks Programme within the Heritage Lottery Fund, gave hope to the beleaguered Gardens and their supporters. A consortium put together a bid for funds. This was successful and the Gardens received £5.06 million, provided that the applicants raised 25 per cent matched funding of about £1.25 million.

After twenty years of fundraising and three generous legacies, a new building named The Dorothy Fox Education Centre was finally completed and opened by the Duke of Devonshire in 2017. The Centre is the focus of a programme for all ages, designed to oversee the development of botanical and horticultural education.

Alison Hunter, Volunteer Historian for the Friends of Sheffield Botanical Gardens (FOBS). Alison completed the Certificate in Botanical Illustration at The University of Sheffield in 2003.

The plants and their profiles

Acer griseum (Franch.) Pax

Family: Sapindaceae

Acer griseum is an attractive, small, slow-growing deciduous tree, with coppery-brown bark that peels away from the trunk but does not fall immediately to the ground. It is known as the paperbark maple. The opposite leaves are made up of three leaflets on short stalks; the margins of the leaves have large rounded teeth. In the autumn the leaves turn from green to a warm reddish-brown colour. The meaning of *Acer* is maple tree and *griseum* means grey, a reference to the colour of the downy underside of the leaves.

The tree was originally described by the French botanist Adrien René Franchet who worked at the Natural History Museum in Paris. Franchet was well known for his taxonomic work on the flora of China and Japan, which was based on plants collected by French missionaries, one of whom was Père Paul Guillaume Farges.

Farges, a missionary and a naturalist, was sent to China in 1867, where he enthusiastically collected plant specimens, many of which were later described by Franchet. He is reputed to have collected over 4,000 specimens in eleven years. In 1892 he collected *Acer griseum* near Chengkou and in 1894 Franchet described the plant as a variety of Japanese maple, which he called *Acer nikoense* var. *griseum.*

Ernest Henry Wilson arrived in Hong Kong from Britain in 1899. He collected many of the plants that Farges had recorded, including the Japanese maple, *Acer griseum*. Wilson worked at the Birmingham Botanical Gardens before becoming a student at Kew under the Director, William Turner Thistleton-Dyer. Thistleton-Dyer recommended him to the Veitch Nurseries for a proposed visit to China. On the way to China he visited the Arnold Arboretum in America where he met the Director, Charles Sprague Sargent.

Wilson introduced *A. griseum* into Britain as seed in 1901. Germination of the seed at the Veitch Nurseries was very successful and in 1907 it was introduced to the Arnold Arboretum in the form of two seedlings. Most trees in Britain and the US today originate from the Veitch collection. An Irish botanist, Augustine Henry, was also thought to have collected *A. griseum* in China. Henry had studied medicine and Chinese and worked as a customs officer in Central and Western China.

The naming of *A. griseum* in 1902 is attributed to Ferdinand Albin Pax, a German botanist. He was assistant to the German botanist Heinrich Gustav Adolf Engler, who was Professor of Botany and Director of the Botanical Garden in Berlin. Pax described several species of plants and animals.

A. griseum is a handsome ornamental tree; it is suitable for a small garden and received an Award of Garden Merit from the Royal Horticultural Society in 1936. The seeds are not always viable and can be difficult to germinate by non-horticultural specialists. The small yellow-green flowers are pollinated by insects and hang on downy stems in small groups. Winged fruits, which are dispersed by wind, turn from green to brown as they dry.

Acer griseum
Artist: Sheila Stancill
Graphite pencil and watercolour
Accepted to the Archive 2006

30'
X5
X5

Aesculus hippocastanum L.

Family: Sapindaceae

The horse chestnut, named *Aesculus hippocastanum* by Carl Linnaeus, is a familiar plant in Britain, found in parks and gardens. It is native to the Balkan Peninsula, Albania, Bulgaria and Greece. The first reference to the plant appeared in the sixteenth century, in a letter from physician Willem Quackelbeen to physician and naturalist Pietro Andrea Mattioli. Quackelbeen explains that the common name for the tree derives from the practice of horses being given three or four of the trees' hard seeds in order to give relief from equine chest ailments.

In the early seventeenth century Lord Wootton, who lived at St Augustine's Abbey in Canterbury, employed John Tradescant to lay out the formal gardens. In 1621 he sent Tradescant on an expedition to Algeria as a 'gentleman volunteer'. The official purpose of the expedition was an offensive against the Barbary pirates, who were causing havoc in the Mediterranean. The intention of sending Tradescant was for him to bring back new plants and indeed he returned with a number of plants, including the seeds of the horse chestnut which he 'obtained' from the cargo of the Barbary pirates. By 1633 a horse chestnut was recorded growing in Tradescant's London garden. A horse chestnut was also recorded growing in the Oxford Physic Garden in 1648, but it had disappeared from records by 1658.

In 1790, a horse chestnut was found growing in the Pindus mountain range in Greece. It was discovered by John Hawkins, a wealthy landowner from Cornwall, who was interested in travelling. Hawkins' claim to have found a horse chestnut was not taken seriously as at that time it was believed to be native to regions much further east. However, many years later in 1879 Theodor von Heldreich, Director of the Botanical Gardens in Athens, confirmed Hawkins' discovery. Visits to the region had been difficult for many years due to various uprisings, but when Heldreich arrived in the area described by Hawkins he saw, to his surprise, a group of horse chestnut trees covered with half-ripe fruit, on the rocky outcrops of a ravine.

The horse chestnut tree is considered to be a short-lived ornamental species, which starts to decline after about 150 years. The wood is regarded as weak but can be used for items such as handles, boxes, fruit racks and kitchen utensils.

Horse chestnuts can be found in parks and private gardens and also by roadsides and in hedgerows. The leaves are palmate and opposite with five to seven leaflets. They appear in the spring emerging from large, shiny, sticky buds. The flowers are white and bell-shaped, held in upright panicles known as candles. They are a rich source of nectar and pollen and are pollinated by both insects and the wind. In autumn, after the leaf has fallen, a leaf scar can be seen in the shape of a horseshoe with nail holes. The fruits are green and spiky and contain one or two seeds; these are known as conkers and used for a popular children's playground game.

Aesculus hippocastanum
Artist: Jo Edwards
Coloured pencil
Accepted to the Archive 2003

a
b
c
d
x2
e
x2
f
x2
g
x2
h
x2
Jo Edwards

Arbutus unedo L.

Family: Ericaceae

Arbutus unedo was described by Carl Linnaeus in 1753 in *Species Plantarum*. The specific epithet *unedo* is attributed to Pliny the Elder, who is reputed to have said after eating the fruit, '*unum tantum edo*', which translates as 'I eat only one'. This statement is thought to refer to the bitterness of the fruit. *A. unedo* is commonly known as the strawberry tree, taking its name from its strawberry-like red fruits. It is in the family Ericaceae, commonly known as the heath or heather family.

A. unedo was discovered growing wild in Killarney, south-west Ireland and around the Mediterranean. In its native habitat it grows at the edge of woodland and on rocky hillsides and can be found as a small evergreen tree or shrub. As a tree *A. unedo* can grow from four to ten metres high, with red to silver-grey smooth bark which is quite distinctive. The bark peels away in long strips to show an attractive copper-red colour underneath. The short-stalked alternate leaves are leathery and simple. They are dark green and glossy on the surface and usually have serrated edges. When the leaves first emerge, they have an attractive red margin.

The flowers appear in late autumn to early winter, with five sepals and five petals. The petals are normally white, although occasionally they can have a pink tinge. They are joined at the base to form a small bell-shaped corolla with a narrow opening. The flowers hang in pendulous clusters or panicles made up of ten to thirty individuals. Pollination is by insects, including honeybees and bumblebees which forage for pollen and nectar. The flowers can be self-fertile and the attractive fleshy spherical fruits ripen in the following autumn. They hang in groups and change colour from green through yellow to red as they mature. The outer skin of the fruit is warty with small protuberances. Birds eat the fruits and disperse the seeds.

A. unedo is grown as an ornamental tree and has a faint but pleasant smell. Some young trees are particularly susceptible to frost and cold dry winds. If the frost is severe, they can die back to ground level, but they quickly regenerate from the roots. *A. unedo* is often grown in urban areas because of its tolerance of atmospheric pollution. It is a useful tree for planting by the sea as it can act as a wind barrier and is salt-tolerant. In some Mediterranean areas *A. unedo* has been used for reforestation after fire as its large root system helps to stabilize the soil.

Pollen dating from Irish bogs suggests that the seeds of the strawberry tree arrived in Ireland over 4,000 years ago, around the same time as the migration of the Beaker people to Ireland from Iberia. The wood from *A. unedo* can be used for burning as firewood and to make charcoal. In Irish mythology it is thought to have protective powers against flooding.

Arbutus unedo
Artist: Barbara Munro
Graphite pencil and watercolour
Accepted to the Archive 2015

a.
x6
b
x6
to 10m
c
x12
d
x6

Banksia marginata Cav.
Protea subvestita N.E. Brown

Family: Proteaceae

The Proteaceae family is large and diverse. It is represented in the Florilegium Archive by *Banksia marginata*, found in south-east Australia, and *Protea subvestita*, found in South Africa.

The Banksias were named after Sir Joseph Banks by Carl Linnaeus in 1782. The epithet *marginata* refers to the slightly curved margins on the underside of the leaves. *B. marginata* was first described by Antonio José Cavanilles in 1800; he was a Spanish taxonomic botanist who was the Director of the Royal Botanic Garden in Madrid. The botanist Robert Brown described further collections as separate species, but in 1870 George Bentham reclassified them all as a single species.

B. marginata is known as the silver banksia. Its native range is New South Wales, Victoria and Tasmania. It is found in forests, scrub, heathland and moorland. The plant is variable and grows mainly as a shrub in the wild. The leaves are narrow and the flower spike is yellow. Pollination is thought to be by small mammals at night and birds by day, looking for nectar. *B. marginata* does not set seed well but the plant can survive fire, partly through the suckering habit of the roots. The seeds are formed inside 'cones'. Heat from fire is required for the 'cones' to open. Once the winged seed is released it can be dispersed by scattering and by birds. *B. marginata* was grown at Kew in 1802.

Protea have different shapes and forms. They were named in 1735 by Carl Linnaeus after the Greek god Proteus who knew about the past, present and future. Proteus would avoid divulging his knowledge by changing his shape to deter people from recognizing him. In South Africa the flower has become a symbol of diversity and transformation.

P. subvestita grows in South Africa and Lesotho. The epithet *subvestita* means partly covered and refers to the hairs on the leaves which are present in the young plants but disappear as the plant matures. The English name for *P. subvestita* is waterlily sugarbush. It is an evergreen shrub with cream to pink flower bracts, some edged with silky white hairs. The plant has both male and female parts in the same flower. The styles are long, becoming thin at their tips which bend outwards on opening. The unscented flower is pollinated by nectar-feeding sunbirds and sugarbirds, which are attracted by its colour. Other pollinators include the protea beetle, *Trichostetha fascicularis*. The fruits take a number of months to ripen and can remain on the plant for several years. Dispersal of the seed occurs after fire when the seed-heads open and the seeds are scattered or blown from the plant. *P. subvestita* seeds have long hairs to facilitate wind dispersal. The hairs also help the seed become attached to the ground where they provide a conduit for transmitting moisture to the seed. Winter rain triggers germination. *P. subvestita* was recorded in 1901 by Nicholas Edward Brown, who was the chief assistant in the Herbarium at the Royal Botanic Gardens, Kew.

Banksia marginata
Artist: Barbara Munro
Watercolour and graphite
Accepted to the Archive 2019

Protea subvestita
Artist: Arnolda Beynon
Graphite pencil and watercolour
Accepted to the Archive 2004

Callicarpa bodinieri var. *giraldii* 'Profusion'

Family: Lamiaceae

Callicarpa bodinieri var. *giraldii* 'Profusion' is an ornamental garden plant, developed to produce numerous bright violet-coloured berries. This cultivar received an Award of Garden Merit from the Royal Horticultural Society. The original species, *C. bodinieri*, has an interesting collecting history; it was found by different botanists over a number of years and given different names. It was first discovered by Augustine Henry in 1887; its native range is southern China to Indo-China.

In the late 1890s seed was sent by Giuseppe Giraldi, an Italian missionary and plant collector, to the German botanist Hermann Albrecht Hesse, who grew the plant in his nursery situated near Weener, on the Ems River. Hesse called the plants *C. giraldiana* after the plant's collector, but the name was not officially recorded.

Callicarpa comes from the Greek word *kallos* meaning beauty and *karpos* meaning fruit: consequently, it is known as the beautyberry. The specific epithet *bodinieri* is named after Émile-Marie Bodinier, a French missionary and botanist who was the first person to describe the plant during his time in China. The plant was received in America by Alfred Rehder at the Arnold Arboretum. Rehder, who was born in Germany, was undertaking research at the Arnold Arboretum and was persuaded by the Director, Charles Sprague Sargent, to work on a comprehensive study of woody plants. During this time Rehder recorded the plant as *C. giraldii*. Seed was introduced from Szechwan into Britain in 1907 by Ernest Henry Wilson. The resulting plants were eventually recorded as *C. giraldiana* by Camillo Carl Schneider, a German botanist and landscape gardener. A French botanist and missionary, Augustin Abel Hector Léveillé, was approached by the botanist Adrien René Franchet on his return from India to describe the plants that were arriving by the shipload from Asia. Léveillé described around 2,000 new species, including *C. bodinieri*, in 1911.

The beautiful cultivar *C. bodinieri* var. *giraldii* 'Profusion' has soft slightly hairy branches and opposite leaves. The leaves are reddish-green when they are young, turning green in the summer and returning to bronze-purple in the autumn before turning a golden yellow. The insignificant lilac flowers are clustered together and develop from the leaf axils. The berries are produced in bead-like groups and last well into winter. Botanically the fruits are drupes, each containing one seed.

C. bodinieri var. *giraldii* 'Profusion' can be pruned to shape to form a neat deciduous bush. If allowed to grow it will become a tall upright shrub, reaching up to three metres in height. The flowers are pollinated by bees, butterflies and other garden insects. To ensure a profusion of berries it is recommended that several plants should be grown together. The berries remain on the plant until late winter, when they may be eaten by birds which help to disperse the seed.

Callicarpa bodinieri var. *giraldii* 'Profusion'
Artist: Julie Mason
Graphite pencil and watercolour
Accepted to the Archive 2015

a)i x3
a)ii x3
b)
c)

Camellia 'Winton' (*cuspidata* × *saluenensis*)
Camellia japonica 'Betty Sheffield'
Camellia japonica 'Anemoniflora'
Camellia sinensis (L.) Kuntze
Camellia 'Mandalay Queen' (*reticulata* hybrid)

Family: Theaceae

The genus *Camellia* was named by Carl Linnaeus in honour of Georg Joseph Kamel, a seventeenth-century pharmacist and naturalist who was known for his work on Chinese plants. Linnaeus used the Latin version of Kamel's surname, Camellus, for the genus name *Camellia*.

Camellias are native to southern China and adjoining countries, where they grow in coastal areas, on scrubby hillsides, in wooded areas and in rainforests. They are evergreen shrubs and have simple, glossy green, leathery, alternate leaves; some have leaves with serrated edges. In the wild the flowers are typically coloured pink, white or red. Several of the tropical species are yellow.

Camellias arrived in Britain in the late seventeenth or early eighteenth century, sent by a physician, James Cuninghame, during his collecting expeditions to China. Cuninghame was highly praised for the plants he had collected and he received sponsorship to return to China several times. Some of the plants were given to Leonard Plukenet, botanist to William III, and to the botanist William Sherard in Oxford. Cuninghame also collected animals and commissioned over 800 paintings by Chinese artists of useful plants, many of which are now in the British Library. After an eventful period abroad, which included being imprisoned for two years, Cuninghame decided to return home. He sailed from Bengal in 1709 on a ship called the *Anna*; tragically, the *Anna* disappeared and was eventually assumed lost at sea.

In 1739 Robert James Petre of Thorndon Hall, Essex was the first person in Britain to bring a camellia into flower from seed. Camellias were thought to be exotics which needed nurturing in order to survive English winters, so Petre grew the seeds in vast hothouses. After Petre's early death from smallpox, his Head Gardener James Gordon set up a nursery in London and was the first person to sell camellias commercially.

Enthusiasm for camellias became widespread when it was realized that they could mostly be grown outdoors. Competitions and camellia shows became popular and camellias were divided into several types based on the form of the flower. Included in the many flower types are Single, which has a single row of up to eight regular or irregular petals with stamens visible in the centre. Semi-Double flowers have two rows or more of regular or irregular petals with prominent stamens. Irregular Semi-Double flowers are like the Semi-Double but may have petaloid structures among the stamens. Formal Double flowers have many rows of petals which are fully imbricated and may have a central cone which does not open, and the stamens are hidden. Elegans, also known as the anemone form, has flowers with large flattish outer petals and a central mass of raised petaloid structures and stamens. Informal Double, or peony form, has flowers with a mass of raised petals and petaloid structures, where the stamens may not be visible.

A revision of the genus *Camellia* was undertaken by the botanist Joseph Robert Sealy in 1958 when eighty-two species were described. In 1984 Hung-ta Chang and Bruce Bartholomew recognized 200 species. Revisions of the number of species in the genus continue to be published.

C. 'Winton' (*cuspidata* x *saluenensis)*
Artist: Pamela Furniss
Graphite pencil and watercolour
Accepted to the Archive 2006

C. japonica 'Betty Sheffield'
Artist: Rosalind Timperley
Graphite pencil and watercolour
Accepted to the Archive 2009

C. japonica 'Anemoniflora'
Artist: Rosalind Timperley
Graphite pencil and watercolour
Accepted to the Archive 2012

C. sinensis
Artist: Neelam Modi
Graphite pencil and coloured pencil
Accepted to the Archive 2012
(The tips of *C. sinensis* are used for the beverage tea)

C. 'Mandalay Queen' (*reticulata* hybrid)
Artist: Rosalind Timperley
Graphite pencil and watercolour
Accepted to the Archive 2013

Carpinus betulus 'Fastigiata'

Family: Betulaceae

Carpinus betulus, the common hornbeam, is native to Europe and Iran. It was described by Carl Linnaeus in *Species Plantarum* in 1753, and can be found growing in woodland in the south of Britain.

C. betulus has strong and durable hard wood, comparable in strength to oak. The Romans used the wood to build chariots and it has also been used for cogs, coach wheels, waterwheels and cartwheels. Charcoal made from the wood was used for smelting iron. In Kent hornbeam charcoal was used to dry the hops, which was part of the brewing process, in oast houses or hop kilns. Hornbeam trees were subject to pollarding and coppicing for hop poles on a long rotation over a number of years. More recently the wood has been used for the striking hammers in pianos, for butchers' blocks, parquet floors and for chess pieces. In America a related species, *C. caroliniana*, is known as the ironwood or musclewood tree.

Hornbeams are in the birch family, Betulaceae. There are several species and cultivars. The different species can be distinguished from each other by comparing the shape of the wing or bract of the fruit and by comparing the appearance of the bark. In the common hornbeam it is pale grey and fluted. The leaves are green and simple with a serrated edge, and are arranged alternately on the branch. The secondary veins are parallel and the leaf surface looks furrowed. The edges of the leaves have a double tooth, with larger teeth between smaller ones. Occasionally there can be confusion between hornbeam and beech. Comparing the leaves can help with identification, the leaves of beech being smoother, darker and glossier than hornbeam and the margin is undulating with shallow teeth. The buds are also different, with beech having long pointed buds whilst hornbeam has shorter stouter buds.

The flowers of the hornbeam, which are produced in the spring, hang in pendulous catkins. The male and female flowers are on separate catkins and are wind-pollinated. The hop-like fruits hang in clusters. The fruit is a small nut, surrounded by a leafy bract with three lobes, which becomes papery as it matures and dries. The shape of the fruit causes it to spin when it falls in windy conditions, enabling the seed to be dispersed away from the parent plant. The tree is attractive to wildlife and in the south of England it has been observed that the nuts are eaten by hawfinches.

The cultivar *C. betulus* 'Fastigiata' is a pyramidal, medium-sized tree with upright branches tapering at the top. It is an ornamental tree often grown as an architectural specimen in large gardens and in parkland. It can be used in an avenue to provide a screen, or planted as a hedge. In the autumn the leaves change to a glowing golden colour. *C. betulus* 'Fastigiata' has been given the Royal Horticultural Society's Award of Garden Merit (AGM).

Carpinus betulus 'Fastigiata'
Artist: Pamela Furniss
Graphite pencil and watercolour
Accepted to the Archive 2011

< 15m
< 12m
♀
A.
♂
B.
× 2.0
♂
C.
♀
× 2.0
G.
D.
E.
♀
F.
2.
1.
× 2.5

Castanea sativa Mill.

Family: Fagaceae

Castanea sativa, the sweet chestnut, was described in the *Gardeners Dictionary* in 1768 by Philip Miller, a Scottish horticulturalist who became Superintendent at the Chelsea Physic Garden in 1722. It was believed that the tree was introduced to Britain by the Romans. However, recent archaeology led by Rob Jarman at the University of Gloucestershire has disproved this theory. Re-examination of archaeological records, new dendrochronology, DNA and historical analysis have not found any evidence that the Romans grew *C. sativa* in Britain. It is likely that the remains of any nuts dating from Roman times were imported with other exotic foods.

The native range of *C. sativa* spreads from Iberia to the Caucasus and it has been widely cultivated across Eurasia. The earliest medieval sites in Britain show it was introduced from north Portugal and north-west Spain. The earliest written records for this introduction appeared in the twelfth century when it was grown in the Forest of Dean and in Monmouthshire for its nuts, honey and durable wood. In the seventeenth and eighteenth centuries the plant was reintroduced from south-west France and Italy. The wood of *C. sativa* is similar to oak but not as strong. It was coppiced to produce hop poles, supports for vines and cleft chestnut fencing. It makes good firewood, but it was mostly used to produce charcoal for ironmaking. Thin planks of *C. sativa* are steam-treated and used to make traditional Sussex garden trugs. The wood splits easily and it is resistant to rot.

C. sativa is a very long-lived deciduous tree; records show it can live up to 700 years. It can be recognized by its deeply fissured and netted bark, which sometimes spirals as the tree matures. On younger trees the bark is smoother. Mature trees can develop vast girths and grow to over 30 metres in height. The lower boughs droop to reach the ground; when they touch the soil they are able to produce roots enabling new trees to generate. The tree has large, alternate, green leaves with variably serrated saw-like edges. The leaves are arranged spirally on the branch and turn golden yellow in the autumn. *C. sativa* has creamy yellow male and female flowers produced on long spikes which emit a noticeable pungent odour. The female flowers are at the base of the spike with numerous male flowers above. The tree cannot self-pollinate and pollen is dispersed by both insects and wind. The fruits, known as nuts, have a glossy reddish-brown ovary wall, and are enclosed in a cup-like shell with an outer spiny protective surface.

The nuts are used across Europe to make flour which is high in protein and gluten-free. In Britain it is a tradition to roast chestnuts, particularly in the winter months. The fruits do not fall far from the tree, so the tree relies on mammals and birds for dispersal: some chestnuts are eaten immediately whilst others are buried, allowing a few to germinate.

The sweet chestnut should not be confused with the horse chestnut *Aesculus hippocastanum* whose fruits, known as conkers, are poisonous.

Castanea sativa
Artist: Rosalind Timperley
Graphite pencil and watercolour
Accepted to the Archive 2016

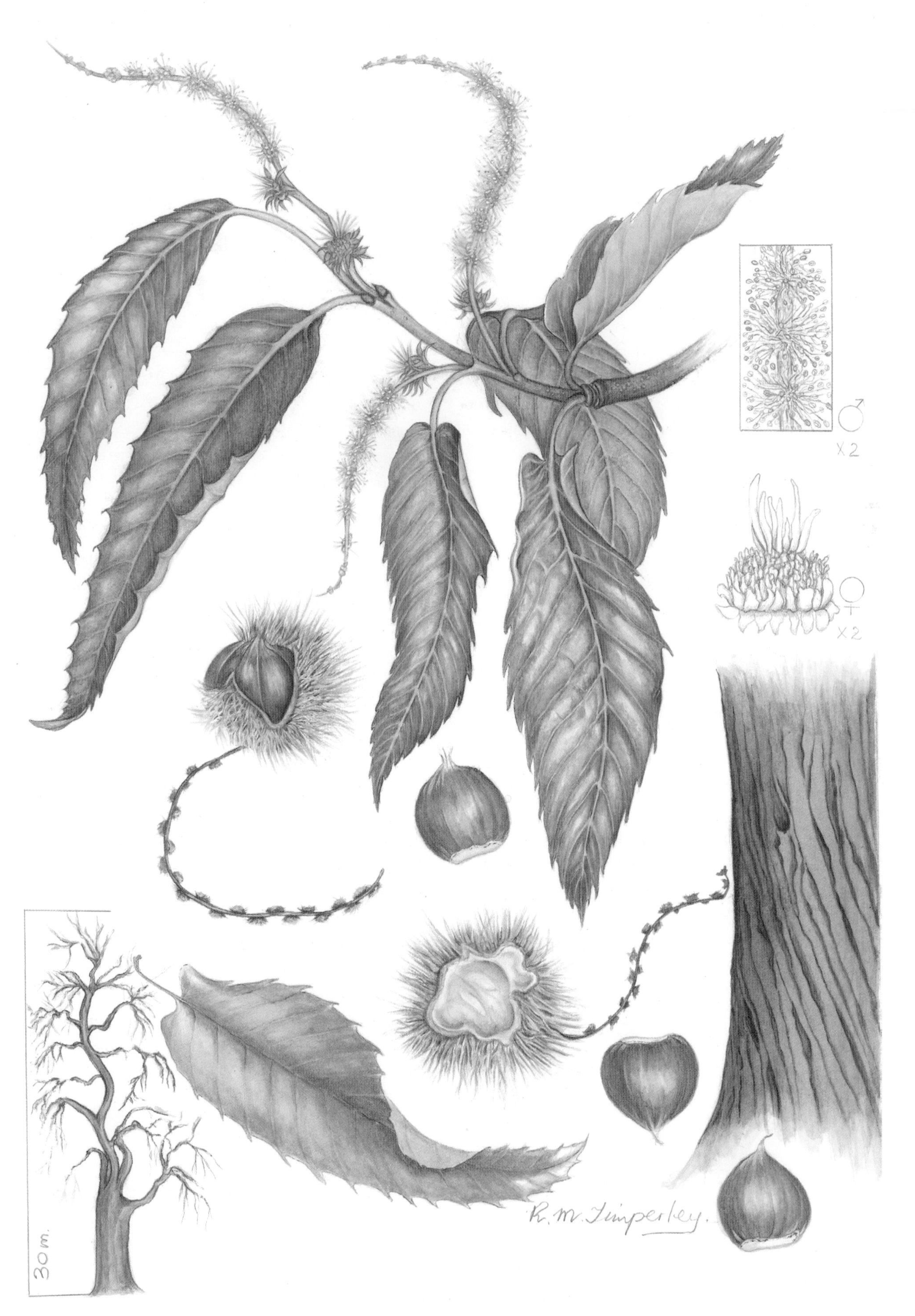
♂
X2
♀
X2
30 m.
R. M. Timperley.

Cedrus atlantica (Glauca Group) 'Glauca'

Family: Pinaceae

The blue Atlas cedar, *Cedrus atlantica* 'Glauca', is a forest tree found in widespread stands in the Atlas Mountains of Algeria and Morocco. Giuseppe Manetti, who died in 1817, is acknowledged to have first discovered and described the Atlas cedar. Manetti was an Italian architect and botanist who designed the first English-style garden in Florence.

After leaving the University of Oxford in 1811, a wealthy young gentleman, Philip Barker-Webb of Milford House, Surrey, went on a collecting expedition. His father had died, leaving Philip a large fortune which enabled him to take up his ambition to travel and to follow up his studies in botany and geology. On his return from his early travels, Barker-Webb spent some time at home in Surrey planting his garden and studying, before setting off again in 1827 for Gibraltar and Tangier. He was keen to explore the interior of the Atlas Mountains but found it almost impossible. Whilst he was in Tangier, he was shown a branch from a native tree from the mountains' interior; the tree was later named the blue Atlas cedar. This is the first known record of the plant to be found by a British collector. Following his extensive travels and plant collecting, Barker-Webb bequeathed his herbarium containing 300,000 specimens to the Natural History Museum in Florence. He died in England in 1854.

In the 1840s, seeds of the Atlas cedar were gathered by Charles, third Earl Somers, and planted at Eastnor Castle, Herefordshire. A tree still growing in the grounds is the earliest known specimen of *C. atlantica* 'Glauca'. In 1855, the Atlas cedar was described by Stephan Friedrich Ladislaus Endlicher, an Austrian botanist and Director of the Botanical Garden in Vienna. It was reclassified by a French botanist Élie Abel Carrière, who based his classification on the original description by Giuseppe Manetti.

C. atlantica is a large, evergreen coniferous tree, endangered in its natural habitat by uncontrolled logging and over-grazing. The blue-grey form *C. atlantica* 'Glauca' grows naturally in the wild; it is more popular as an ornamental garden plant than *C. atlantica* because of its distinctive blue-grey colour. Seeds of *C. atlantica* 'Glauca' were grown in France and clones were distributed in 1867; the clones were like *C. atlantica* 'Glauca' but slightly smaller.

The cultivar *C. atlantica* (Glauca Group) 'Glauca' has a vertical trunk, the branches becoming horizontal as they mature. The leaves are in the form of blue-grey needles which are produced singly and grow spirally on spur shoots, forming whorls at the ends. Male and female cones are produced separately. Male cones shed their pollen in the autumn. The females develop into smooth, flat-topped, barrel-shaped cones which turn from green to brown as they mature. They have closely wrapped scales, each with two seeds. After two to three years the cones disintegrate on the tree and the winged seeds are dispersed. The cones contain a resin which is distasteful to squirrels.

C. atlantica has been used for its timber. Essential oils extracted from its foliage and bark are used in the medicinal and perfume industries. Oils extracted from blue Atlas cedar wood were used by the ancient Egyptians for embalming.

Cedrus atlantica (Glauca Group) 'Glauca'
Artist: Sheila Stancill
Graphite pencil , watercolour and pen and ink
Accepted to the Archive 2004

Cercis siliquastrum L.

Family: Fabaceae

Cercis siliquastrum is in the family Fabaceae, the pea and bean family. It was originally discovered in dry woodlands and on warm stony slopes, from France through to the eastern Mediterranean. The name *Cercis* was given to this plant by the Greek botanist Theophrastus. The name describes the resemblance of the dark, dried, flat fruits to a weaver's shuttle. The second part of the name, *siliquastrum*, was applied by Carl Linnaeus in his *Species Plantarum* in 1753, and again refers to the fruit. The word comes from the Latin *siliqua* which means a pod and *astrum* which means partial likeness.

Theophrastus was born about 370 BCE. He was a philosopher and botanist and successor to Aristotle. His name was originally Tyrtamus, but it is believed that it was changed to Theophrastus by Aristotle to reflect his god-like manner and elegant speech. Theophrastus inherited Aristotle's books and created a botanic garden. He is known for two scholarly botanical treatises, an *Enquiry into Plants* and the *Causes of Plants*. He was the first person to attempt to systemize plants and became known as the Father of Botany.

Legend is that Judas Iscariot hanged himself from the *C. siliquastrum* after his betrayal of Jesus Christ; in response, the flowers turned from white to red with shame. However, it is more likely to have been known as the tree of Judea because it grew profusely around Jerusalem.

C. siliquastrum is regarded as an ornamental tree in Britain. It has alternate, heart-shaped, deep purple leaves in the spring, which gradually turn to green in the summer months. They change again in the autumn to become a variety of colours from bronze to yellow. As they die, they have a noticeable toffee aroma. The deep purplish-pink flowers are pea-like and grow in clusters on stalks from the branches of the tree, usually before the leaves appear. Sometimes the flowers appear from the bare trunk, a condition known as cauliflory which is often found in tropical plants; cauliflory enables insects that cannot fly to reach the flowers. The flowers provide a rich source of nectar for bees, which help with pollination by carrying pollen produced by the stamens on their bodies from flower to flower. Fruits are in pods and they have numerous seeds. The pods stay on the tree for some time after the leaves have fallen but they can be dislodged by strong winds.

The tree has a symbiotic relationship with certain bacteria in the soil and can fix atmospheric nitrogen in its root nodules. It can use nitrogen for its own growth, but its presence can also be beneficial to other plants growing alongside. The wood of *C. siliquastrum* is hard and attractively grained and it has been used for veneers. In North America another species, *C. canadensis*, and cultivars of it, are known as redbuds.

Cercis siliquastrum
Artist: Jo Edwards
Coloured pencil
Accepted to the Archive 2004

ai
aii
aiii x2
b x2
c
d
JVE

Chaenomeles speciosa 'Moerloosei'
Chaenomeles × *superba* 'Rowallane'

Family: Rosaceae

Chaenomeles speciosa, the flowering quince, is native to China but can be found in Bhutan, Burma and Korea. The plant was cultivated for many years in Japan before being introduced to Western Europe.

In 1784 a plant found growing in the mountainous area of Hakone in Japan was named *Pyrus japonica*. It was described by Carl Peter Thunberg, who thought it was related to a pear. Twelve years later in 1796 *P. japonica* was introduced into Britain by Joseph Banks, who mistakenly believed that his plant was the same as the one Thunberg had named. However, it was discovered that this plant was from the original Chinese species. When the mistake was discovered it was renamed *P. speciosa*.

In 1807 Christiaan Hendrick Persoon, who studied medicine at Leiden and Göttingen, recognized that *P. japonica* did not belong to the genus *Pyrus*, mainly because it had numerous seeds. He placed it in the genus *Cydonia*, the quince family, and it became known as *Cydonia japonica*. In 1818 the English botanist and horticulturalist Robert Sweet renamed the plant Banks had introduced as *Cydonia speciosa*. John Lindley looked at the fruit again in 1822 and placed the plant in a newly established genus *Chaenomeles*. The name *Chaenomeles* means gaping apple or apple that splits. It comes from the Greek words *chaino* to split and *meles* referring to apple. Takenoshin Nakai, a Japanese botanist, published the name of the Chinese plant as *Chaenomeles speciosa* in 1929.

Around 1870 the Bristol nursery of W. Maule & Son introduced to Britain another flowering quince which was found growing wild in Japan. Many years later it was discovered that this was the true *Pyrus japonica* originally described by Thunberg. A third species, introduced from China to Europe, was thought to be simply a variety of *C. speciosa*, but it is now considered to be a different species and is named *C. cathayensis*. The genus consists of three species: *C. japonica*, *C. speciosa* and *C. cathayensis*.

C. speciosa 'Moerloosei' is an attractive cultivar, named for the Belgian horticulturalist Moerloose by Adolf Papeleu. It is a deciduous spreading plant of medium height. The simple green leaves are alternately arranged and have serrated edges. Pink buds open to reveal the flowers which have five white petals tinged with pink. They have the appearance of apple blossom and the plants are sometimes known as *C. speciosa* 'Apple Blossom'. Bees pollinate the flowers and the fragrant fruits are shaped like small, hard, yellow-green apples, often used decoratively by florists.

C. × *superba* is a chance hybrid between the species *C. speciosa* and *C. japonica* which appeared in nurseries around 1898. *C.* × *superba* 'Rowallane' was selected as a chance seedling in 1920 by Hugh Armytage-Moore who inherited Rowallane Gardens, Northern Ireland in 1917: the new cultivar was given the name 'Rowallane' after the place where it was found.

Chaenomeles speciosa 'Moerloosei'
Artist: Caroline Holley
Graphite pencil and watercolour
Accepted to the Archive 2011

Chaenomeles × superba 'Rowallane'
Artist: Barbara Munro
Watercolour and graphite
Accepted to the Archive 2017

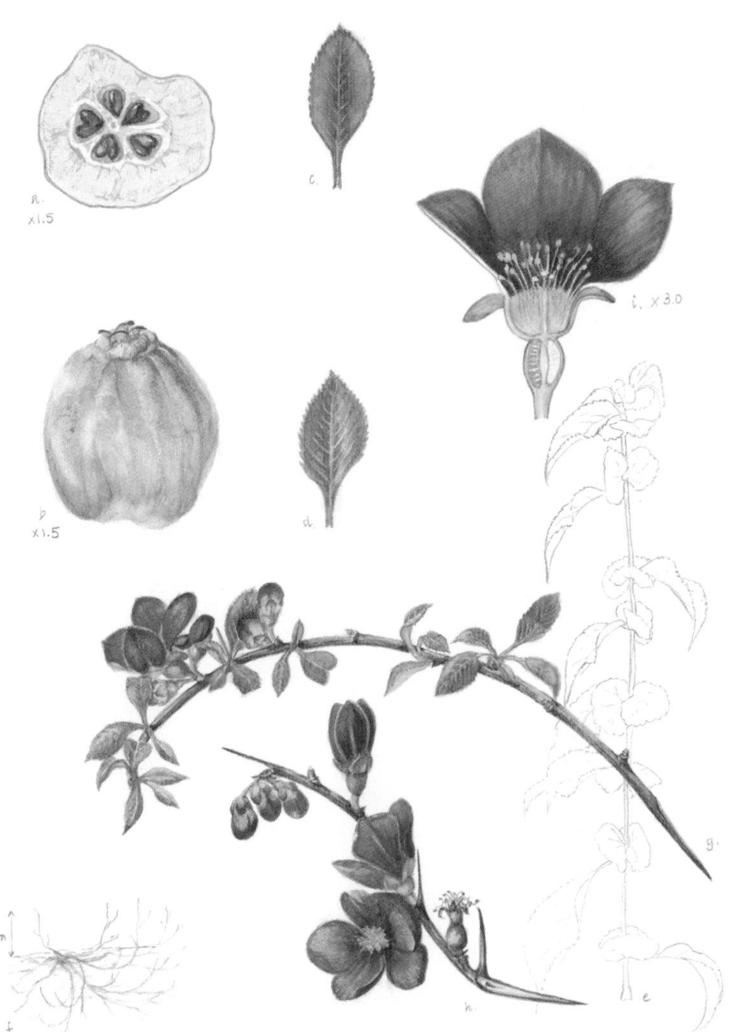

Citrus trifoliata L.

Family: Rutaceae

Citrus trifoliata was named in 1763 in *Species Plantarum* by Carl Linnaeus. It is known as the Japanese bitter orange and is in the family Rutaceae. *C. trifoliata*'s native range is central and south China. An illustration of the plant appears in *Amoenitatum Exoticarum* published in 1712 by German physician and naturalist Engelbert Kaempfer. Between 1683 and 1693 Kaempfer visited Russia, Persia, Arabia, India and South-East Asia. He became the medical officer for the Dutch East India Company and in this capacity was sent to Japan. Kaempfer collected, studied and drew plants, learnt the Japanese language and gained the respect and assistance of the people he met. Kaempfer may have seen *C. trifoliata*, which was introduced from China, growing in gardens in Japan.

In 1838 the plant was reclassified as *Poncirus trifoliata* by the naturalist Constantine Samuel Rafinesque, who was born in Turkey in 1783, the son of a French father and German mother. Rafinesque named nearly 3,000 genera but less than fifty are accepted today. He was considered to be eccentric and his work became controversial. Later, when the 'Principle of Priority' was applied, many of Rafinesque's contributions were excluded. The Principle of Priority recognizes that the first scientific name to be given to a plant is correct.

C. trifoliata was introduced to Britain by Robert Fortune, the Scottish plant hunter. Fortune was first employed as an apprentice gardener for a Mr Buchan at Kelloe, Berwickshire. In 1840 he gained a position at the Royal Botanic Garden, Edinburgh under William McNab, who supported his application for the post of Superintendent of the Hothouse at the Horticultural Society's garden at Chiswick. Not long after he had secured this post Fortune applied for the position of the Society's Collector in China; he made three visits to China and one to Japan.

C. trifoliata is a slow-growing ornamental shrub or small tree. It is deciduous and has large, visible, green thorns on stout green shoots. Occasionally thorns emerge from the bark, which is dark grey-brown with green photosynthetic stripes. The branches are not straight and develop in a zigzag pattern which eventually forms a web; this structure makes *C. trifoliata* a good hedging plant and in the US it has been used as a stock fence. The alternate, green leathery leaves usually have three, occasionally four or five, leaflets with a winged stalk. The middle leaflet is slightly larger than the two outer leaflets. When they are crushed, they release a spicy smell. The leaves turn yellow with a slight tinge of orange in the autumn. Fragrant five-petalled white flowers, which are hermaphrodite, appear in the spring; they are larger than those of true citrus plants. The stigma and anthers are yellow. *C. trifoliata* flowers are pollinated by insects but can also self-pollinate. Green fruits ripen to a dull yellow and resemble a small bitter orange with a downy surface and numerous seeds. The plant is hardier than other types of citrus and in Britain it can be grown outside in frost-free areas.

Citrus trifoliata
Artist: Sally Strawson
Graphite pencil and watercolour
Accepted to the Archive 2010

Clematis armandi Franch.

Family: Ranunculaceae

The native range of *Clematis armandi* is from central to south China, Myanmar, Tibet and Vietnam. The genus name *Clematis* is from the Greek word *klema* meaning vine branch and refers to its vine-like habit. It is named after Jean Pierre Armand David, a French missionary.

David was a younger son and not in line to inherit from his father so, as was customary for many younger sons, he joined the clergy. He became a priest and was sent to teach at a school in Italy where he was very popular and instilled a love of nature in the students. In 1862 after ten years' teaching, David had become a reputed and respected naturalist. He was sent to China with instructions from the French government to collect specimens for the Jardin des Plantes and for the Muséum national d'Histoire naturelle in Paris. During three lengthy expeditions David sent a vast and important collection of specimens to Paris. He undertook his last expedition in the 1870s.

In 1874 Louis Édouard Bureau, who was a French physician and botanist, was appointed to a post at the Muséum national d'Histoire naturelle in Paris to organize the classification of plants. In 1875 he became the Director of the Herbarium and in 1880 the French botanist Adrien René Franchet was appointed as his assistant. Franchet was instructed by Bureau to describe the collection of plants that had been deposited in the Herbarium by David. In 1881 David met French missionary and botanist Pierre Jean Marie Delavay in Paris. He encouraged Delavay to continue his collecting work in China, which the latter did until 1890, adding some 200,000 specimens to the Herbarium.

Ernest Henry Wilson introduced *C. armandi* into Britain in 1900 during his first expedition to China for the Veitch Nurseries. He called at the Arnold Arboretum on the way to study methods of collecting, storing and shipping seeds and plants.

C. armandi is an attractive, ornamental, evergreen climbing plant. It has large leathery, glossy green leaves with entire edges, which appear to fall downwards in a cascade. The leaves are ternate, the middle leaf being larger than the ones either side. New leaves are bronze in colour before turning a dark glossy green. There are clusters of four to six scented flowers; the white or creamy-white petaloid sepals can be variable in shape on different plants. The star-shaped flowers appear on new growth and have an almond-like smell which drifts on the wind, the scent being more noticeable in warm weather; the flowers have numerous stamens and cream anthers. Bees and other insects visit the flowers for pollen and nectar. The fruit is a cluster of plumed achenes, each of which holds one seed: these are dispersed by wind.

C. armandi is vigorous and can be trained against a wall or fence. It climbs by twisting its petioles or leaf stems around a support. It can be pruned back to control its size after flowering, allowing it time to establish new growth before the next flowering season. Old plants can be cut down to the base and will quickly regenerate.

Clematis armandi
Artist: Sheila Stancill
Graphite pencil and watercolour
Accepted to the Archive 2005

Clivia miniata (Lindl.) Verschaff.

Family: Amaryllidaceae

In 1815 the naturalist William John Burchell returned to England with new plants he had collected from South Africa. Many of these plants arrived as dried herbarium specimens. Burchell spent the following years describing the plants and naming them. The collection included a plant later known as *Clivia miniata*.

In the early 1820s James Bowie, a gardener and plant collector from the Royal Botanic Gardens, Kew, sent home new plants collected from the same area as William Burchell. One of the plants collected by James Bowie was named *Clivia nobilis* by John Lindley who was assistant to the Horticultural Society and supervised the collection of plants at its garden in Chiswick. The plant was named in honour of Lady Charlotte Florentia Clive who became the wife of the third Duke of Northumberland. The duchess was an enthusiastic plantswoman from a plant-loving family and she had a particular interest in South African plants. The name was in recognition of Lady Clive's ability to cultivate the plant and bring it into flower in her conservatory at Syon House, which lay across the river from the Royal Botanic Gardens, Kew.

A few years later more South African plants arrived in England and a new plant similar to *Clivia nobilis* was named *Vallota speciosa* by John Lindley. This plant was successfully cultivated by James Backhouse, a nurseryman in York. In 1854 Backhouse exhibited the new plant at the Horticultural Society in London where it caused some interest among the botanists and horticulturalists who were undecided whether it was related to *C. nobilis* or *V. speciosa*. Lindley gave it the name *Vallota miniata*. However, William Hooker, with whom Lindley was acquainted, called the new plant *Imantophyllum miniatum* and it took several years before the confusion was settled. Finally, it was agreed that all the plants were the same and they should be called *Clivia miniata*.

In 2018, Graham Duncan of the National Biodiversity Institute at Kirstenbosch National Botanical Garden, South Africa corrected the name to *C. miniata* (Lindl.) Verschaff. Through his research Duncan discovered that Ambroise Verschaffelt was the first to transfer *Vallota miniata* to *Clivia* in 1857. *C. miniata* has a number of common names including the Natal lily and bush lily. These showy plants became very popular house plants with the Victorians.

C. miniata is an evergreen perennial which has beautiful, tubular, bright orange flowers with a yellow throat. There can be as many as twenty flowers at the top of a long, strong, straight stem. In Britain they usually flower from spring to summer. The fruits colour from green to red as they ripen. The plants are clump-forming, with several bright green, glossy, strap-like leaves which emerge from stocky rhizomes. A plant was introduced to the pavilions at Sheffield Botanical Gardens in 2002.

Clivia miniata
Artist: Mary Acton
Graphite pencil and watercolour
Accepted to the Archive 2015

M Acton.

Cornus kousa subsp. *chinensis* (Osborn) Q.Y. Xiang

Family: Cornaceae

The family Cornaceae contains mainly trees and shrubs. They are known as dogwoods and were originally discovered in Korea, Japan and China in the nineteenth century. Dogwoods are usually deciduous; they are popular garden plants and have stunning autumnal foliage and fruits. In the winter they have colourful stems and bark and some have large attractive bracts in the summer.

C. kousa was recorded in Japan by Heinrich Bürger, a German biologist and botanist. In 1825 he was appointed by the Dutch government to go to Japan as assistant to Philipp Franz von Siebold, a German physician and botanist who had founded a medical school in Nagasaki. Siebold's students helped him by collecting plants for him to study from areas where travel by Europeans was restricted. Siebold also employed experienced Japanese hunters to collect specimens and he cultivated the plants that would survive in the Dutch climate in his small garden. Many of the plants were illustrated by Japanese artists. Bürger gave him invaluable help with record keeping and he later became Siebold's successor.

Collecting in China in the mid-nineteenth century was Henry Fletcher Hance, a British diplomat who was first posted to Hong Kong in 1844. Hance was later appointed to the post of senior assistant at the British Consulate in Canton and then became vice-consul at Whampoa. For more than forty years he collected and described Chinese plants in his spare time, eventually becoming a leading authority on the local flora. He met the Irish botanist Augustine Henry and other collectors when they visited China. He advised on how to protect specimens from insect damage and how to properly prepare and preserve herbarium specimens. Augustine Henry collected plants in Badong and it was there that he discovered *C. kousa*.

In 1907, when collecting seed for the Arnold Arboretum in Boston, Ernest Wilson collected *C. kousa* near Yichang in China. The plant had larger bracts and leaves than the Japanese form and was named as a variety and called '*chinensis*'. Wilson introduced the plant to Britain. It was also found in northern Assam in 1950 by botanist and plant collector Frank Kingdon-Ward who brought it back to England as seed.

C. kousa subsp. *chinensis* is a striking plant. The greenish-yellow flowers are surrounded by four stalked whitish-green bracts which gradually change to cream. They become tinged with pink at the edges as the plant matures as shown in the illustration. The compound fruit is like a red strawberry and appears in the centre of the pink-tinged bracts in the autumn. The leaves are dark green with wavy edges, blue-green on the underside and turning a deep purplish-red in the autumn.

This attractive plant was introduced to Sheffield Botanical Gardens in the 1960s. The plant is named *Cornus kousa* subsp. *chinensis* (Osborn) Q.Y. Xiang, to comply with the International Plant Name Index (IPNI) and the Flora of China project.

Cornus kousa subsp. *chinensis*
Artist: Mary Acton
Graphite pencil and watercolour
Accepted to the Archive 2005

Corymbia ficifolia (F. Muell.) K.D. Hill & L.A.S. Johnson

Family: Myrtaceae

Corymbia ficifolia is an ornamental Australian tree, which was formerly known as *Eucalyptus ficifolia* but was transferred from the genus *Eucalyptus* to *Corymbia* in 1995. The new genus, *Corymbia*, was recognized by botanists Kenneth D. Hill and Lawrence Alexander Sidney Johnson, working on a revision of the eucalypts at the Royal Botanic Garden, Sydney.

The name eucalyptus comes from the Greek *eu* meaning well and *calyptos* meaning covered and refers to the operculum, the structure which protects the flower before it opens. The first records show that in 1770 Joseph Banks and Daniel Solander collected specimens of eucalyptus on an expedition to Australia. On Banks's third visit in 1777, a specimen was collected which was named *Eucalyptus obliqua* by the French botanist Charles-Louis L'Héritier de Brutelle. From 1788 more species were collected, many of which were named by the botanist James Edward Smith. In 1797, after examining specimens collected by botanist Luis Née, a separate genus *Angophora* was published by the Spanish botanist Antonio José Cavanilles.

Ferdinand Jacob Heinrich von Mueller, who became Director of Melbourne Botanic Gardens, co-operated with George Bentham, who was President of the Linnaean Society, to work on Bentham's *Flora Australiensis* in which a number of eucalypts were described. Bentham based himself at the Royal Botanic Gardens, Kew and worked entirely from dried specimens brought from Australia. By 1866 von Mueller and Bentham had named 149 species of eucalyptus based on the characteristics of the anthers. As research progressed and became more sophisticated, the classification of eucalyptus became increasingly complicated.

Corymbia refers to the clusters of flowers which arise from one stem to form a flat-topped cluster or corymb; the individual flower stems grow at different lengths to create this effect. The specific epithet *ficifolia* comes from the Latin, *ficus* meaning fig and *folium* meaning leaf. It refers to the similarity to leaves of some species found in the genus *Ficus*.

C. ficifolia is a prolific flowering tree and is known as the red-flowering gum. However, the colour of the flowers can vary from white to pink to orange. *C. ficifolia* has barrel-shaped fruits and winged seeds. The fruits are known as gum-nuts and are attractive to some birds; the dark brown seeds are spheroid. Flowers are pollinated by nectar-loving birds and insects, including parrots and bees. The simple leaves are dark green, slightly glossy on top and pale green underneath. The bark is grey-brown and rough.

C. ficifolia produces a lignotuber, a swelling at the crown of the root. The swelling, which can be seen at the base of the tree, is formed as protection for the tree against fire. If the tree is not able to photosynthesize through loss of its leaves in a fire, it can use starch from the lignotuber to survive. Buds in the lignotuber are able to develop into new stems. The tree, which is not frost-tolerant, is native to Western Australia and grows in open forests in restricted south coastal regions.

Corymbia ficifolia
Artist: Helen Fitzgerald
Graphite pencil and watercolour
Accepted to the Archive 2010

Helen Fitzgerald 2010

Cyclamen coum Mill.

Family: Primulaceae

Cyclamen are perennial plants, members of the Primulaceae family. They can be found in the wild in coastal areas of the Black Sea from East Bulgaria via Turkey and the Caucasus to the Crimea. Another group can be found bordering the north-east of the Mediterranean and into the mountains from Turkey to Israel. *Cyclamen coum* grows with *Helleborus orientalis* and *Primula vulgaris* along the shores of the Black Sea. As a woodland plant it grows in rocky areas and at higher altitudes. *C. coum* is thought to have reached Western European gardens by the seventeenth century, where it was used medicinally and also cultivated as an ornamental plant. The species was described by Philip Miller in the eighth edition of the *Gardeners Dictionary* published in 1768. Miller was a gardener at the Society of Apothecaries Garden at Chelsea; he was appointed by Sir Hans Sloane and highly regarded for his botanical and horticultural knowledge.

The genus name *Cyclamen* is thought to have derived from the Greek word *kyklos* meaning circle, referring either to the rounded tuber or to the way in which the stem of the fruit twists round in a circle. The specific epithet *coum* is thought to refer to Coa or Koa, an eastern region of ancient Cilicia, now the southern coast of Turkey, where *C. coum* was found.

C. coum naturalizes freely and grows just beneath the surface of humus-rich soil. The rounded heart-shaped leaves have smooth edges or are very slightly toothed. They are fully developed by the time the flowers appear. The plants vary from those with plain green leaves to others with attractive silver patterns as shown in the illustrations. The underside of the leaves varies in colour from light green to magenta. The flower stalks of *C. coum* emerge directly from the tuber which is round and brown and flattens out as it matures. The white to deep pink flowers appear in winter or early spring and are usually unscented. The petals are reflexed and have a dark red blotch near the mouth of the corolla. The flowers are morphologically adapted to buzz pollination; pollen is expelled at a precise frequency generated by the wings of a variety of insects. As the fruit develops, the stalk begins to coil, bringing the fruit, which is a five-chambered capsule, nearer to the ground. When it is dry the capsule splits open and the seeds spill out; these are carried away and dispersed by ants, attracted by their sugary coating. The ants eat the testa, the seed coat or covering, and dispose of the seed, usually some distance from the parent plant.

C. coum is a variable species which continues to confound botanists and horticulturalists. It is endangered through the over-collection of the tubers for the horticultural trade and by climatic change affecting the wild population.

Cyclamen coum
Artist: Jenny Harris
Graphite pencil and watercolour
Accepted to the Archive 2003

Cyclamen coum
Artist: Jane Howell
Graphite pencil and watercolour
Accepted to the Archive 2004

Cyclamen coum
Artist: Jenny Harris
Graphite pencil
Accepted to the Archive 2005

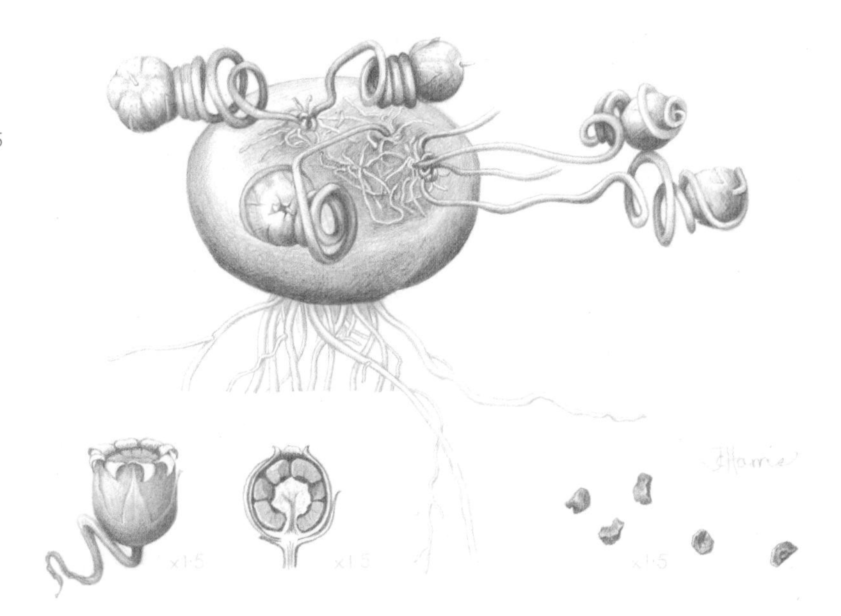

Daphne bholua Buch.-Ham. ex D. Don

Family: Thymelaeaceae

Daphne bholua is a flowering shrub which grows in the wild from eastern Nepal to south-central China. In the wild it is evergreen at lower altitudes and deciduous at higher levels. The plant was first recorded in 1825 in a book called *Prodomus Florae Nepalensis*, which was edited by Scottish botanist David Don and featured the collections of Francis Buchanan-Hamilton and Nathaniel Wallich.

Buchanan-Hamilton was a Scottish physician and botanist who studied at the University of Edinburgh. He became Surgeon to the Governor General of India, Richard Colley Wellesley, in 1803, and was appointed head of the Institution for Promoting the Natural History of India in 1804; this institution was founded by Wellesley. Later, from 1814–15, he was appointed Superintendent at the Calcutta Botanic Garden; he collected and described many new plants in the region including *D. bholua*.

Don's father, George Don, was a curator at the Royal Botanic Garden, Edinburgh. Through an introduction to the Scottish botanist Robert Brown, initiated by his father, David Don worked at the Society of Apothecaries Garden (now the Chelsea Physic Garden). Later, he became Librarian and Keeper of the herbarium of Aylmer Bourke Lambert, who was a founding fellow of the Linnaean Society. Don retained these posts when in 1822 he succeeded Robert Brown as the Librarian to the Linnaean Society.

D. bholua is in the family Thymelaeaceae, which mainly consists of trees or shrubs. The family was established by a French botanist, Antoine Laurent de Jussieu, who published a system of natural classification that was considered an improvement on the system published by Linnaeus.

D. bholua is a flowering, ornamental, evergreen shrub. The first flowers do not appear until after about three years' growth but nevertheless it is a popular winter plant in British gardens and has a wonderful scent. The dark green, simple leathery leaves are mostly alternate and narrow with smooth edges. The corolla of the flower is formed by four sepals with the lower parts fused into a tube; this arrangement imitates the absent petals. There are two stamens to each sepal, making eight stamens altogether arranged in two whorls with one set above the other. The flowers are pollinated by insects and bees. The fruit is a black, fleshy berry with one seed. Studies have shown that birds help disperse the seeds in the wild. The seeds are only viable for a short period of time and need to be sown soon after collection. All parts of the plant are poisonous, although it is used in Chinese medicine to treat various conditions.

In the Himalayas the bark is used for making paper and has the advantage of having long fibres which naturally stick together. Once the pulp is prepared it is dried on a frame in the sun. *D. bholua* is known in the region as the Nepalese paper plant. The inner layers of bark fibres are used to make rope.

Daphne bholua
Artist: Mary Morton
Graphite pencil and watercolour
Accepted to the Archive 2018

Dianella tasmanica var. *variegata* C. Pyneart

Family: Asphodelaceae

Dianella tasmanica var. *variegata* was described in 1903 by Charles Pyneart, a Belgian nurseryman. The variety *variegata* refers to the creamy-white and green variegation of the strap-like leaves.

D. tasmanica is native to south-east New South Wales and Tasmania. It is named after Diana, the Roman goddess of hunters and the countryside; *ella* means small. The specific epithet refers to the plant's native origin, Tasmania. The plant is also known as the blue flax lily, because the small blue flowers resemble the simple blue flowers produced by some members of the flax family.

The first recorded specimen of *D. tasmanica* was collected in Tasmania in 1837 by South African Ronald Campbell Gunn, a naturalist and plant collector who was living in Tasmania and working as a government official. It was first described in 1858 in *Flora Tasmaniae* (1855–60) by Joseph Dalton Hooker: the book is an account of Hooker's travels in Tasmania (formerly Van Dieman's Land) where he stayed for six months in 1840/41, during a voyage with Sir James Clark Ross on his Antarctic expedition. He joined HMS *Erebus* in 1839 and stayed until the voyage ended in 1843. *Flora Tasmaniae* included descriptions of all the plants found in Tasmania. Hooker dedicated it to Gunn and William Archer as both men had assisted him in finding native plants.

Gunn was a correspondent of Joseph's father, William Hooker. They were introduced by Robert Lawrence who had developed an interest in botany through his friendship with William Hooker in Britain. Lawrence went to Tasmania in 1825 to join his family who had settled there around 1822–23. William Hooker recruited him as a collector in 1830 and Lawrence sent plant specimens to Hooker at Kew. Lawrence died in 1833 when he was only twenty-six years old, long before Joseph Hooker arrived in Tasmania in 1840.

William Archer was a naturalist who was born in Tasmania; he studied architecture and surveying in London before returning to Tasmania in 1842. He was in England again pursuing studies in botany from 1856 to 1858. When he returned to Tasmania, he sent botanical specimens and illustrations of new plants he had discovered to the Hookers at Kew.

D. tasmanica var. *variegata* can be grown outside in most areas in Britain, but it is not frost-tolerant. Alternatively, it can be grown as an indoor pot plant in a cool greenhouse or conservatory. The plant forms grass-like mounds and the leaves have finely serrated edges. The branching underground rhizome enables the plant to spread. It is suitable for the edge of a woodland garden in dappled shade.

The slender flowering stems have a panicle of delicate flowers at the top which have reflexed sepals when they are mature. Insects pollinate the flowers. The fruit is a beautiful glossy steel-blue trilocular berry with a few black shiny seeds. In its native habitat the seeds are dispersed by birds, including parrots, which eat the fruit.

Dianella tasmanica var. *variegata*
Artist: Judyth Pickles
Graphite pencil and watercolour
Accepted to the Archive 2010

×2
×½
×2

Elegia mucronata (Nees) Rchb. ex Kunth

Family: Restionaceae

The Restionaceae family, known as restios, are a diverse family of mainly reed-like grasses found in the Western Cape of South Africa. The genus name *Elegia* means a song of lamentation and could refer to the sound of the plants as they sway in the wind. The specific epithet *mucronata* means pointed or prickly. From fossil records restios appear to have been around during the Cretaceous period. They grow in tussocks in sandy soil in areas near the sea and at higher levels. The early Dutch settlers named the area where the restios grow as the *fynbos*, which means fine bush and refers to the large number of bushy plants with small fine leaves growing in the area.

Restios dominate much of the Cape Floristic Region. Other families that are native to the area include the Proteaceae and Ericaceae. The plants are sometimes destroyed by fire but can regenerate from seed. Horticulturalists from Kirstenbosch Botanical Gardens in South Africa have been collecting restio seed over a number of years in order to promote the horticultural value of the plants. At first, they had problems with germination, but research helped to understand how germination is brought about through 'plant-derived' smoke, which can break dormancy.

Christian Gottfried Daniel Nees was the first to publish a description of *E. mucronata* in 1830; he called it *Restio mucronatus*. Nees was a German physician and botanist who described about 7,000 plant species. In 1841 Carl Sigismund Kunth described the restio as *E. mucronata*; he was a German botanist who became interested in botany after meeting Alexander von Humboldt, a Prussian naturalist and explorer. Kunth became Humboldt's assistant and classified the plants he collected. Kunth named *E. mucronata* on behalf of Heinrich Gottlieb Ludwig Reichenbach, based on the original name and the description by Nees.

Reichenbach was a German botanist who studied medicine and natural science at the University of Leipzig. He became Director of the State Museum of Zoology in Dresden and was well known for his connection with Leopold Blaschka. It was Reichenbach who invited Blaschka to make a set of marine invertebrates in glass, which led to the famous Blaschka collection of glass flowers which can be seen at the Harvard Museum of Natural History in the US.

E. mucronata grows in damp areas in sunny open positions. Male and female flowers are on separate plants and they are wind-pollinated. Plants of *E. mucronata* have long strong stems known as culms. The leaves have been reduced to a golden papery sheath and the flowers are in spikelets. Some species of restios, brought into cultivation, are available in Britain. The plants can be propagated by division, just before new shoots emerge from the ground. They are popular with florists for their architectural structure and long-lasting seed heads.

Elegia mucronata
Artist: Cathrine Allsopp
Graphite pencil and watercolour
Accepted to the Archive 2005

Enkianthus campanulatus (Miq.) G. Nicholson

Family: Ericaceae

Enkianthus campanulatus was first described by Friedrich Anton Wilhelm Miquel, who was a Dutch botanist and Professor of Botany at the Universities of Amsterdam and Utrecht. He was the Director of the National Herbarium at Leiden from 1862 and published over 7,000 botanical names. The genus name is from the Greek *enkyos* which means pregnant and *anthos* meaning flower and refers to the rounded shape of the lower part of each flower. The specific epithet *campanulatus* comes from the Latin for bell-shaped, and again refers to the flower.

In 1877 Charles Maries was sent by the nurserymen Veitch & Sons for three years to search for new hardy plants in Japan and China. He sent many beautiful plants back to England, including *E. campanulatus* which is native to northern Japan where it grows on open mountain slopes from Hokkaido to Honshu and Shikoku. Collecting trips by Maries were fraught with difficulties. On one occasion he arranged for his collection of seeds to be taken to Hakodate for shipment to England, but the ship was laden with seaweed causing it to run aground. The box containing the seeds was transferred to another vessel which capsized and sank; tragically the seed collection was lost. Maries had to retrace his steps to replace the collection; this time the seeds arrived safely in London. Maries returned to England in 1880 and his herbarium was sent to the Royal Botanic Gardens, Kew.

The plant was reclassified by George Nicholson in 1885, when he updated the original description by Friedrich Anton Wilhelm Miquel into modern botanical systematics. Nicholson was the son of a nurseryman and started work at the Fisher & Holmes nursery at Handsworth, Sheffield. He worked for a time at a nursery in Paris and in 1873 returned to England to start working at Kew. In 1886 he was appointed Curator and lived at Kew with his son, his sister acting as his housekeeper. He wrote a number of articles about cultivated trees and shrubs; his most important work was his contribution to *The Illustrated Dictionary of Gardening* published in 1882, which became a standard reference work. He was elected a fellow of the Linnaean Society and awarded the Veitch Memorial Medal for services to gardening. Nicholson was also awarded the Victoria Medal of Honour in recognition of his contribution to horticulture. He retired in 1901 due to ill-health.

E. campanulatus flowered in 1889 at Veitch's Coombe Wood Nursery in London. It was brought to the attention of Joseph Dalton Hooker, editor of *Curtis's Botanical Magazine*, and drawn by his second cousin Matilda Smith. Matilda's drawing was lithographed for the magazine by John Nugent Fitch, a nephew of Walter Hood Fitch. Encouraged by Hooker, Matilda Smith became the main artist for the magazine and contributed over 2,300 illustrations over thirty years.

E. campanulatus is a small, upright, deciduous shrub which prefers acid soil. It has bell-shaped, nodding flowers which hang in pendulous groups; the fruit is a capsule. The young shoots are reddish and the finely toothed leaves produced in a cluster at the end of a twig are mid-green. In the autumn the leaves turn a bright coppery red.

Enkianthus campanulatus
Artist: Sue Nicholls
Graphite pencil and watercolour
Accepted to the Archive 2003

10·0 mm
10.0 mm

Eranthis hyemalis (L.) Salisb.

Family: Ranunculaceae

Eranthis hyemalis, the early-flowering winter aconite, was probably introduced to Britain in the late sixteenth century. In his herbal of 1596 Gerard describes the plant as being 'counted to be very dangerous and deadly'. He stated that the deeper the snow through which the flower emerged, the larger the flower.

Matthias L'Obel, a Flemish physician, described the plant in *Stirpium Adversa Nova* which was published in 1571. He was one of the first to use the similarity of leaf shape to relate plants to each other and suggested that related plants would have similar medical properties, thus assuming *E. hyemalis* would be deadly poisonous, as it was similar to plants in the genus *Aconitum* such as monkshood and wolfsbane. He also recorded the plant in *Plantarum Seu Stirpium Historia* published in 1576.

The genus name is from the Greek *er* meaning spring and *anthos* meaning flower. The specific epithet *hyemalis* is from Latin and means winter-flowering. A common name for the plant in the mid-seventeenth century was winter aconite or winter wolfsbane. In 1616 Andrea Cesalpino, an Italian botanist, published a classification of plants based on their flowers, fruits and seeds rather than on their leaf shapes and medicinal properties. His work was influential in the systematic work of Carl Linnaeus. Another name for the plant was *Cammarum hyemale*, which was included in Dr John Hill's *The British Herbal* printed in 1756.

E. hyemalis was described in the transactions of the Linnaean Society by Richard Anthony Salisbury in 1807. Salisbury, born in 1761, was a botanist who studied at the University of Edinburgh. It is thought he may have been instructed by Professor John Hope who was a physician and botanist. Hope followed the Linnaean system of classification and was well known for his work on plant classification and physiology. Although Salisbury undertook valuable work in botanical sciences, he was involved in several disputes and ignored by some of his contemporaries. In 1809 Salisbury was appointed the first Honorary Secretary of the Royal Horticultural Society, but came under criticism for leaving the accounts in disarray.

E. hyemalis is a clump-forming herbaceous perennial, native to the deciduous woodlands of Europe, including lowlands and rocky places. Its native range is from southern France to Bulgaria, the Balkans, Turkey and Iraq. It was first recorded in the wild in Britain in 1838, and is now naturalized. Once established it spreads quickly. The plants develop from tuberous rhizomes and have solitary flowers consisting of five to eight glossy yellow sepals. The flowers are surrounded by a green whorl of dissected bracts; the basal leaves emerge separately. There is a ring of nectaries between the stamens and the sepals. Pollination is by early insects, bees and flies. The carpels develop into fruits with large brown seeds which scatter on drying. Horticulturally, it is a popular ornamental plant for the winter garden.

Eranthis hyemalis
Artist: Vivienne Taylor
Graphite pencil and watercolour
Accepted to the Archive 2003

Eranthis hyemalis
Artist: Valerie Oxley
Graphite pencil and watercolour
Accepted to the Archive 2006

Fothergilla major (Sims) Sweet

Family: Hamamelidaceae

Fothergilla major is in the witch hazel family, Hamamelidaceae. It is known as the mountain witch alder and is native to the south-east of the US. The plant is named after John Fothergill, a Quaker physician and botanist. In 1762 Fothergill bought Upton House in Essex and created a botanic garden to grow his large collection of North American and rare plants from around the world. He noted that the North American plants grew well in peat under a north wall. The name *F. major* was published by Robert Sweet in 1818. Sweet was a horticulturalist and botanist who worked as a gardener from the age of sixteen and was associated with nurseries in Stockwell, Fulham and Chelsea. The physician and botanist John Coakley Lettsom, a protégé of Fothergill, published a catalogue of all the plants in Fothergill's garden after his death.

Fothergill was a patron of the botanical artist and Quaker Sydney Parkinson. In 1768 Parkinson went with Captain James Cook and botanists Joseph Banks and Daniel Solander on a voyage to the South Seas on board HMS *Endeavour*. In 1773 Fothergill supported the American botanist William Bartrum, also a Quaker, on his travels to the south-east of North America – Carolina, Georgia and Florida. In return Bartrum sent Fothergill his journal of the expedition, including specimens and drawings. When the journey ended in 1777, Bartrum asked Fothergill if Dr Solander could be asked to identify the collection and publish descriptions. Unfortunately, this request was not fulfilled because Solander was busy with the collections from the South Seas voyage of Cook and Banks. Fothergill died in 1780 and Solander in 1782. In 1788 Bartrum was still trying to discover what had happened to the collections he sent to London. It appears that Banks purchased some of Bartram's specimens after Fothergill's death and they became part of the collections at the British Museum (Natural History).

One of Fothergill's correspondents was Dr Alexander Garden, a Scottish physician who lived in South Carolina. In his spare time Garden was a plant collector and sent specimens of the plants he found to John Ellis in England and Carl Linnaeus in Sweden. He collected a species of *Fothergilla* which Linnaeus named as *F. gardenii*. It is not known who introduced *F. major* to England but it was in cultivation in 1780 at the time of Fothergill's death. It fell into obscurity, but was reintroduced to the Royal Botanical Gardens, Kew in 1902 by botanist Charles Sprague Sargent, the Director of the Arnold Arboretum at Harvard University.

F. major is a deciduous shrub, whose stems, buds and leaves are covered with star-shaped hairs, giving them a downy appearance. It has large asymmetrical alternate leaves with slightly toothed edges. In the autumn the leaves turn from russet to a deep yellow. Clusters of scented flowers are made up of numerous white stamens with yellow anthers emerging from a ring of reduced sepals; they are pollinated by bees and other insects. The olive-brown fruits are beaked capsules which expel two shiny black seeds when the fruits are dry. *F. major* has received the Royal Horticultural Society's Award of Garden Merit.

Fothergilla major
Artist: Anne Dent
Graphite pencil and watercolour
Accepted to the Archive 2005

Fragaria × ananassa Pink Panda = 'Frel'

Family: Rosaceae

Fragaria is the Latin name for strawberry and comes from the word *fragrans* meaning fragrant, referring to the aroma of the fruit. *Fragaria × ananassa* is a cross between *F. chiloensis* and *F. virginiana*. Horticulturalists found that they could enlarge the fruit whilst retaining the taste using this new cultivar.

Although strawberries have been written about since the sixteenth century, it was in the eighteenth century that a French botanist, Antoine Nicolas Duchesne, made a special study of strawberries, particularly observing variations and mutations. He created a collection of strawberries at the garden of the Petit Trianon at Versailles. British agriculturalist Richard Weston corresponded with Duchesne and discussed strawberry varieties and variations. Thomas Andrew Knight, President of the Royal Horticultural Society, and Michael Keens, a gardener from Isleworth, were also involved by experimenting with various breeding techniques to enlarge the fruit. Keens was the first to introduce a large strawberry fruit to the Royal Horticultural Society.

Strawberries are known as false fruits; the true fruits are the single seeds which have their own dry seed wall and are embedded in the outside of the swollen receptacle. Once the flower is pollinated and the petals have fallen away, the receptacle at the base of the flower enlarges. The swollen receptacle turns from green to red, to become the fleshy part that is eaten. The flowers are pollinated by insects and the fruits are eaten and dispersed by birds, slugs and humans.

The strawberry plant is an attractive perennial and its addition to the ornamental garden was soon considered worth pursuing. The compact shape of the individual plant, plus its ability to spread by runners, were considered attractive features for ground cover at the front of a border. The colour and size of the flower became an important factor in its development for the ornamental garden, along with the possibility that it could still produce edible fruit. Experiments were undertaken by crossing the cultivated strawberry with the deep pink-purple marsh cinquefoil *Comarum palustre*, formerly *Potentilla palustris*, from a related genus, *Potentilla*, both in the family Rosaceae.

Cultivars produced from these commercial crossings developed into good strong plants with offspring in the form of plantlets at the end of runners or stolons. The new plantlets rooted readily and could be removed from the parent plant once they became established. Horticulturalists found that the plantlets retained the same characteristics and colour as the parent plants.

The toothed leaves of the new cultivars for the ornamental garden are similar to the leaves of the cultivated strawberry. They are green, and are divided into three leaflets with thin stipules at the base of the leaves. In the autumn they turn a colourful red-orange colour. The ornamental cultivars have a succession of flowers, each with five to eight rounded pink petals. Although the fruit is edible it is often removed from ornamental cultivars to encourage more of the attractive pink flowers to develop.

Fragaria × ananassa Pink Panda = 'Frel'
Artist: Sheila Stancill
Graphite pencil and watercolour
Accepted to the Archive 2007

SMStancill 01.

Fraxinus excelsior L.

Family: Oleaceae

Fraxinus excelsior, the common or European ash, is one of Britain's native deciduous trees. It is found growing across Europe from Norway to Turkey. *F. excelsior* was classified in 1753 by Carl Linnaeus in *Species Plantarum*. It is a member of the olive family.

In Scandinavian and British folklore, the common ash, *F. excelsior*, was thought to be a protective tree. Trees were planted near holy wells and many myths and legends circulated about ash having healing properties. It was thought that the tree was a link between heaven and hell: the long trunk was regarded as a conduit between the heavenly world, represented by the head of the tree and its branches, and the underworld, represented by its roots.

The trunk is grey and smooth, but as the tree matures the bark becomes furrowed. The twigs of *F. excelsior* are easily recognizable; they have a terminal cluster of black velvety buds followed behind by paired, alternate, black buds on grey-brown, smooth shoots. The green leaves are pinnate with a terminal leaflet and rows of opposite leaflets behind. The wind-pollinated maroon flowers appear before the leaves emerge. Petalless male and female flowers can be found on different trees or on different branches of the same tree. It has been discovered that an ash tree can change its gender from year to year. The stalked fruits appear in green clusters which turn brown and twist as they dry. They remain on the tree after the leaves have fallen and spiral to the ground when they fall in late winter.

F. excelsior is traditionally a woodland and hedgerow tree; it is also popular in parks and gardens. In the past, it was pollarded to protect the branches from grazing animals and to reduce shade on the ground. It was often underplanted with hazel in coppiced woodland and used for firewood and charcoal.

The wood of *F. excelsior* has a cream to olive-green colour; it is strong and flexible and was used for tools of different kinds including early spears, harrows, ploughs and rakes. More recently it has been used in the manufacture of frames for tennis racquets, skis, oars and billiard cues. It has also been used in the manufacture of small boats, yachts, aircraft wings and car frames for the motor industry. The smooth strong wood is popular for making ladders, free-standing furniture, made-to-measure kitchens and floors. In the eighteenth and nineteenth centuries ash trees were grown in groves for hop poles. In north Nottinghamshire the North Clay hop trade flourished from the eighteenth until the end of the nineteenth century but dwindled after the hops became infected with blight.

Ash dieback disease, which is caused by the fungus *Hymenoscyphus fraxineus*, was first detected in Britain in 2012. Black blotches appear on the leaves of the tree and lesions appear on the branches; infected trees quickly die.

Fraxinus excelsior
Artist: Jo Edwards
Coloured pencil
Accepted to the Archive 2003

a
b
c
d
a(i)
e
a(ii)
x5
d(i)
x5
d(ii)
x5
Jo Edwards

Galanthus nivalis L.

Family: Amaryllidaceae

Galanthus nivalis was described by Carl Linnaeus in 1753 in *Species Plantarum*. The name comes from the Greek *gala* meaning milk and *anthos* meaning flower; the specific epithet *nivalis* means snowy. The common name for this plant is snowdrop. It is not native to Britain but it has become naturalized. The native range of the plant is from the Pyrenees eastward to the Ukraine and from Germany and Poland southwards to Italy, Albania and northern Greece.

G. nivalis can be traced back to the fifteenth and sixteenth centuries. John Gerard refers to a snowdrop in a description of 'bulbous violets' in his herbal of 1597, but it is not until the 1663 revision that the snowdrop is referred to by name: 'some also call them Snowdrops'. It would appear that the snowdrop became naturalized in Britain from garden escapes. There are several references to wild snowdrops in floras such as William Hudson's *Flora Anglica* of 1778 and James Edward Smith's *Flora Britannica* of 1804, where the locations of 'wild' colonies are described.

G. nivalis is a perennial bulbous plant. There are usually two long flat leaves, rarely three or more, which face each other as they emerge from the sheath. The tip of the leaf is strengthened so that it can push through hard frosty ground. The sap contains 'antifreeze' proteins which prevent ice crystals forming, thus helping the plant to survive low temperatures. The central vein on each leaf is prominent on the underside. The flower stalk emerges between the flat leaves with the flower bud upright at its tip, enclosed in a spathe. When the bud has reached its growing height, it pushes through the spathe and hangs downwards on a thin pedicel. The pendulous flowers are protected from adverse weather conditions, but open in the sunshine to allow insects to enter for pollination to take place.

The flower has six perianth segments or tepals: three white, curved, outer segments and three shorter, inner segments. The three inner segments have a notch and green markings on their inner and outer surfaces which are an important identification feature. The flowers are buzz-pollinated: pollen is released through slits in the top of the anther, which opens in response to vibration caused by bees entering the flowers; the same process can be triggered by wind. The inferior ovary has three chambers containing the ovules. When the ovules are fertilized, they and the ovary enlarge and the size and weight pull the capsule downwards until it reaches ground level where it continues to mature. The capsule opens and the seeds are dispelled; they are carried away by ants which are attracted by an oil- and protein-rich appendage on the seed called an elastiome – this is fed to larvae underground. The seed is unaffected and is able to germinate away from the parent plant.

The snowdrop has become a much-loved herald of spring.

Galanthus nivalis
Artist: Valerie Oxley
Graphite pencil and coloured pencil
Accepted to the Archive 2004

x 2½
x 2½
x 2½
x 2
x 2
Valerie Oxley

Gaultheria shallon Pursh

Family: Ericaceae

The first person to describe *Gaultheria shallon* was Frederick Traugott Pursh, a German botanist. He travelled all over North America collecting plants, mostly funded by his patron, the American physician and botanist Benjamin Smith Barton. In 1811 Pursh travelled to England to visit London and to consult the Sherard Herbarium at the University of Oxford. The Sherard Herbarium was the largest in Europe at that time and a large number of specimens were from North America. Pursh was preparing to publish *Flora Americae Septentrionalis*, which described the plants of North America. It was published in 1814 and contained a drawing of *G. shallon* by Pursh. He later suffered ill-health due to alcoholism and died destitute in 1820, aged forty-six.

The genus was named after a French physician, Jean-François Gaultier, who left France in 1742 to live in Quebec. He was a keen naturalist and collected plant specimens which he shipped back to France. The specific epithet *shallon* derives from the Native American Chinook name for this plant.

The introduction of *G. shallon* to cultivation in Britain is attributed to David Douglas, who started work as a boy gardener for the Earl of Mansfield at Scone Palace in Scotland. He progressed to work on the Scottish plant collection at the Glasgow Botanic Gardens for William Hooker. In 1823 Douglas set off on a plant-hunting expedition organized by Hooker for the Royal Horticultural Society of London. He visited the east coast of America where he collected fruit trees as well as a large variety of other plants. In 1824 he set off again, this time to visit the west coast. The first noteworthy plant he found was *G. shallon*. Douglas very quickly learnt enough of the Chinook language to report back that *G. shallon* should be called *G. salal*, not *G. shallon*. He also confirmed that the plant was widely spread through the pine forests. Sadly, Douglas suffered an early death. In 1834 when he was only thirty-five years of age, he fell into a bullock pit whilst climbing Mauna Kea in Hawaii. The pit was used by local hunters to capture wild cattle. Foul play was suspected but not proved and he was initially buried in an unmarked grave. Eventually a stone cairn was erected near to where his body was found.

G. shallon is an evergreen shrub with shiny dark green leaves. The leaves are a lighter green on the underside and slightly rough to touch; they are pointed and finely serrated. There are between five and ten small bell-shaped pink to white flowers, each with five sepals, which hang at the ends of branches. The roundish berries turn from green to blue-black when ripe and are described as edible. The plant has medical properties and the leaves are used in floristry. *G. shallon* was brought into cultivation in Britain as it was thought it would be useful as ground cover for large gardens and for pheasant cover on large estates. In some lowland forest areas in Britain it has become invasive and difficult to eradicate, threatening the regeneration of native vegetation.

Gaultheria shallon
Artist: Sue Nicholls
Graphite pencil and watercolour
Accepted to the Archive 2003

a
Sue Nicholl.
10.0mm
b
c
d
e
f
g

Geranium endressii J. Gay

Family: Geraniaceae

Geranium endressii, or French crane's-bill is a species of hardy geranium. The native habitat of the plant is in the north-west Pyrenees, where it comes into flower over the summer months. The genus name *Geranium* comes from the Greek word *geranós* which means crane. The specific epithet *endressii* comes from the name of a German pharmacist and plant collector, Philip Anton Christoph Endress.

Endress spent two years training as a pharmacist with his uncle Emmanuel Friedrich Hartmann. In 1823 they collected plants around Strasburg where they lived. Endress became an assistant to the botanist Jean François Aimé Théophile Philippe Gaudin in 1827 and he made several visits to the Pyrenees to collect plants for a German scientific society known as *Unio Intineraria*, supported by William I of Württemberg. He died of malaria when he was only twenty-five years old, after returning from his third trip to the Pyrenees. *G. endressii* was described in 1832 by Jacques Étienne Gay, who named the plant in honour of Endress. Gay was a well-known French botanist and taxonomist, born in Switzerland in 1786. When he was young, Gay collected plants in the Swiss Alps under the guidance of the botanist Gaudin to whom Endress had been an assistant.

G. endressii has opposite green leaves divided into five deeply cut lobes. There are stipules at the base of the leaves and the margins are toothed; the leaves have beautiful autumn colouring. The cup-shaped flowers have five slightly notched pink petals and five sepals. They generally appear in pairs from June onwards. The petals have red veined markings and the ovary is superior with five united carpels. Bees pollinate the flowers. The fruit is a schizocarp, which looks like a crane's bill when it is fully developed. When it is dry the beak-like column splits open in strips. The strips spring backwards and upwards launching the seeds which lie in a cup attached to the bottom of the column; the seeds are effectively thrown some distance from the parent plant.

G. endressii has received the Award of Garden Merit from the Royal Horticultural Society. It is a popular garden plant and enjoys most soil types. In the spring it grows into a mound before developing a sprawling habit, spreading outwards. It can be used as ground cover and is happy to be in the sun or part shade; it can be cut back in mid-summer to encourage new growth and divided in the spring or autumn. *G. endressii* can be found as a garden escape on wooded banks and waste land, usually close to habitation.

The country rhyme 'Snakes will not go where geraniums grow' suggests that some geraniums are a deterrent to snakes. It is also said that dreaming of geraniums means that a recent quarrel will come to nothing and will soon be forgotten. These myths apply to geraniums in general and not particularly *G. endressii*.

Geranium endressii
Artist: Lesley Badger
Graphite pencil and watercolour
Accepted to the Archive 2005

Hamamelis mollis Oliv.
Hamamelis × *intermedia* 'Diane'

Family: Hamamelidaceae

Hamamelis mollis, or witch hazel, is an attractive deciduous shrub with scented flowers that appear in early winter. It was first introduced by Charles Maries who started work at his brother's plant nursery near Liverpool. Several years later he joined James Veitch & Sons of Chelsea where he showed an interest in Chinese and Japanese plants. In the spring of 1877 Henry Veitch sent Maries to China on a plant-collecting expedition to explore the Yangtze valley. In 1878, when he was in south-east China, Maries found *H. mollis* and sent seed back to Veitch to propagate at his Coombe Wood nursery. This expedition was a commercial venture, set up to find plants that would become profitable in cultivation. Unfortunately, Maries did not get on well with the Chinese and many of his plants were destroyed; he returned home with very few specimens. *H. mollis* was not formally described at that time.

In 1875 William Turner Thistleton-Dyer was appointed Assistant Director of the Royal Botanic Gardens, Kew, and in 1877 he was given responsibility for an international research laboratory. He suggested that the flora of China should be surveyed as some areas were under-recorded. The work was undertaken by William Botting Hemsley, who became the Keeper of the Library and Herbarium at Kew from 1899 to 1908, and Francis Blackwell Forbes, an American botanist with expertise in Chinese seed-producing plants. Their first reports were published in 1886.

Around this time Augustine Henry was collecting in China and found *H. mollis* near Patung, in Hupeh province. Henry sent material to Kew in 1887 where *H. mollis* was formally described by Daniel Oliver, a botanist who was Librarian of the Herbarium at Kew from 1860 to 1890.

A seedling of *H. mollis*, from the collecting expedition by Charles Maries, survived at Veitch's Coombe Wood nursery, but it had been given the wrong identification. The plant fell into obscurity for twenty years. George Nicholson, a curator at the Royal Botanic Gardens, Kew, was visiting the Coombe Wood nursery and recognized the shrub from specimens he had seen in the Herbarium at Kew, probably from the collections of Augustine Henry.

H. mollis is an ornamental shrub. The bright yellow flowers appear on leafless winter stems; they have four strap-like petals with four stamens surrounded by four hairy sepals. The fruit is a woody capsule which splits open to eject two glossy black seeds, which usually mature about a year after pollination. In the autumn the broad, oval, alternate leaves turn butter-yellow. They are slightly hairy on the top and downy on the underside. The name's specific epithet *mollis*, which means soft or downy, derives from this feature.

Hamamelis × *intermedia* is a hybrid which was first described in 1945, having been found in the Arnold Arboretum. The cultivar 'Diane' was developed in Belgium at the Arboretum Kalmthout. It was described by Robert and Jelene de Belder in 1969. 'Diane' has copper-coloured petals with contrasting dark purple sepals. The beautiful autumn foliage ranges from orange through to red.

Hamamelis mollis (yellow flowers)
Artist: Jane Howell
Graphite pencil and watercolour
Accepted to the Archive 2003

Hamamelis mollis (leaves)
Artist: Jane Howell
Graphite pencil and watercolour
Accepted to the Archive 2005

Hamamelis × intermedia 'Diane'
Artist: Rosalind Timperley
Graphite pencil and watercolour
Accepted to the Archive 2014

Hardenbergia violacea (Schneev.) Stearn

Family: Fabaceae

Hardenbergia violacea is a legume and is in the Fabaceae family. It is a native plant of Australia and grows in the wild in Queensland, Victoria, Tasmania, New South Wales and South Australia. It can be found in a variety of habitats from coastal to mountainous areas, often in open shrubby forests. Bushfires are an important part of the regeneration of plants in these forests, and the roots of *H. violacea* can regenerate after fire. The plant has a number of common names: purple coral pea, happy wanderer, climbing morning glory and false sarsaparilla, among others.

The Dutch botanist and nurseryman George Voorhelm Schneevoogt, who was renowned for being able to grow rare plants from seed brought back by collectors, described the plant in his book *Icones Plantarum Rariorum* which depicted plants at the Voorhelm & Schneevoogt nursery at Haarlem. Schneevoogt named the plant *Glycine violacea*. He published a hand-coloured engraving by Hendrik Schwegman alongside the description.

In 1830 an Austrian diplomat and traveller, Karl Alexander Anselm Baron von Hugel, set off on a six-year plant-collecting expedition to India, Ceylon and Australasia. During 1833 and 1834 he travelled to Western Australia and visited Tasmania and New South Wales. Hugel wrote a 2,000-page diary about his Australian travels, which was translated into English. During his travels he found *G. violacea*. In 1833 he proposed to change the generic name to *Hardenbergia*, after his sister Franziska, Countess von Hardenberg. The specific epithet *violacea* refers to the violet colour of the flowers.

George Thomas Bentham, an English botanist, described the genus *Hardenbergia* in volume 1 of *Flora Australiensis*, which appeared in seven volumes from 1863 to 1878. German-born Ferdinand Jakob Heinrich von Mueller, a botanist who had moved to Australia with his sisters to find a warmer climate for health reasons, assisted Bentham. In 1940 the plant was described again, this time by William Thomas Stearn in the *Journal of Botany, British and Foreign*.

H. violacea is a slender evergreen vine with beautiful pink to deep purple pea-like flowers and simple, leathery leaves with prominent veins. It is generally found as a sprawling plant that can climb by twining its stems around each other to gain height. However, it can be found in the wild as a bushy shrub-like plant. The flowers are made up of five petals: the standard, the keel formed by two fused petals and two wing petals. It is pollinated by insects and the seeds are thought to be dispersed by ants. Rabbits eat the plant, but it is known to be toxic for horses and can cause colic. In the nineteenth century the roots were used by Australian Aborigines to make a soft sweet drink called sarsaparilla; the Aboriginal name for the plant is *waraburra*.

In Britain *H. violacea* can be grown outdoors in mild areas, or as an indoor plant in a conservatory or greenhouse. It has been given the Royal Horticultural Society's Award of Garden Merit and is grown inside the pavilions at Sheffield Botanical Gardens.

Hardenbergia violacea
Artist: Jo Edwards
Coloured pencil
Accepted to the Archive 2005

Hedychium gardnerianum Sheph. ex Ker Gawl.

Family: Zingiberaceae

Hedychium gardnerianum, the Kahili ginger, is an ornamental tropical plant found in the humid lowlands of the eastern Himalayas, northern India, Nepal and Bhutan. It was introduced to the Calcutta Botanic Garden by Edward Gardner. He was the first Resident (an ambassador in all but name) to the Nepal royal court to be appointed by the East India Company; his mission was to improve relations with the Nepalese government.

Dr Mark Watson, Head of Major Floras at the Royal Botanic Garden, Edinburgh has written a profile of Gardner, in which he states that 'life in the Residency for Gardner and his staff was at times tedious'. Gardner began corresponding with Nathaniel Wallich, a Danish surgeon and naturalist who also worked for the East India Company as Superintendent at the Calcutta Botanic Garden. Wallich encouraged Gardner to take an interest in botany and with the help of assistants Gardner began to collect plants and to send specimens to Calcutta. The small team of collectors were soon overwhelmed by the number of plants they were finding and Wallich agreed to send two of his own collectors, Francis de Silva and Bharat Singh, to help. These two men were able to collect outside the restricted area available to Gardner.

Gardner sent nearly 1,000 specimens to Calcutta which were enthusiastically received by Wallich. Although he was only an amateur botanist, Gardner provided Wallich with herbarium specimens as well as living plants.

The citation for the plant is attributed to John Shepherd. Unfortunately, his name has been misspelled as Sheppard in *The Botanical Register* of 1823, causing subsequent confusion; the editor of *The Botanical Register*, John Bellenden Ker Gawler, may have been responsible for this mistake. John and Henry Shepherd were the first two curators of the Liverpool Botanic Garden, which was created by a group of Liverpool botanists led by William Roscoe. The Garden received plants for cultivation from Wallich and it was Wallich who suggested naming *H. gardnerianum* after Gardner. Roscoe became an authority on the Zingiberales order of flowering plants. He used specimens grown at the Liverpool Botanic Garden, including *H. gardnerarium*, to prepare a reorganization of the order.

H. gardnerianum is known for its intoxicating scent. The plant has sturdy perennial rhizomes which produce tall annual pseudo-stems. These stems produce glossy green, lance-shaped, alternate leaves, widely spaced in two ranks. The flowers emerge on a separate stem in the form of a large spike. Pollination is by insects as well as long-tongued butterflies which reach down to the nectaries at the base of the style. The ovary is inferior and the fruit is a capsule with three compartments. The inner surface of the fruit is orange and the bright red sticky seeds are dispersed by birds and small mammals. In New Zealand and Hawaii, where the plant is listed as invasive, the rhizomes create dense areas where other plants are unable to regenerate or become established.

Hedychium gardnerianum
Artist: Anne Dent
Graphite pencil and watercolour
Accepted to the Archive 2008

LIP (MEDIAN STAMINODE)
STIGMA
ANTHER + ENCLOSED STYLE
FILAMENT
COROLLA TUBE
1 OF 2 LATERAL STAMINODES
CALYX TUBE
1 OF 3 COROLLA LOBES
AD

Helianthus mollis Lam.

Family: Asteraceae

Helianthus mollis comes from the Greek words *helios* for the sun and *anthos* for flower. The specific epithet *mollis* means soft and refers to the soft hairs on the front and back of the leaves. It was recorded by Jean-Baptiste-Pierre-Antoine de Monet, chevalier de Lamarck, in 1789.

Lamarck was a French naturalist who followed family tradition and enlisted in the army but after being injured he retired and studied medicine instead. In 1778 he published *Flore Françoise* in three volumes, and from 1778 to 1793 worked as a botanist at the Jardin du Roi in Paris, now the Jardin des Plantes. He was appointed to the Chair of Botany in 1788 and became a member of the French Academy of Sciences in 1779. After his death in 1829 his herbarium, which consisted of 19,000 specimens, was acquired by the Muséum national d'Histoire naturelle in Paris. The herbarium specimens were sent to him by a network of botanists throughout the world over a number of years. Towards the end of his life his eyesight failed and he was unable to continue with his scientific work. He was cared for by his daughter but they became quite poor; his books and house were sold at auction after his death and the family had to apply for financial assistance.

H. mollis was also recorded by Carl Ludwig Willdenow, a German botanist and plant taxonomist who studied botany and medicine at the University of Halle. Willdenow had an early interest in botany and started a herbarium before going to university. In 1794 he became a member of the Berlin Academy of Sciences and in 1801 was appointed a director of the Berlin Botanical Garden, where his herbarium, consisting of over 20,000 specimens, is preserved.

H. mollis is known as the ashy sunflower in the US; it is a perennial plant which grows wild on roadsides and in abandoned fields in the North American prairies. It has become a popular plant in Britain and was used by Professors Nigel Dunnet and James Hitchmough from The University of Sheffield's Department of Landscape Architecture to trial 'prairie planting' before using this style for the highly acclaimed landscaping at the London 2012 Olympics.

H. mollis spreads readily from underground rhizomes and has been used in the US to prevent soil erosion. The flowers are bright yellow and are held high up on erect pink-coloured stems, either singly or in a cluster. There are fifteen to thirty sterile yellow-petalled ray florets and numerous fertile disc florets each holding a single seed. The flowers are pollinated by butterflies, bees and other insects. The whole plant is covered with soft downy hairs which give the leaves a grey-green appearance. The stiff stalkless leaves are opposite and the leaf margins have slightly rounded teeth. A study in the US in 1978 showed this plant has allelopathic properties, which means it can kill or suppress the growth of neighbouring plants.

Helianthus mollis
Artist: Valerie Oxley
Graphite pencil and coloured pencil
Accepted to the Archive 2005

x 6
x 6
x 6
x 2
Valerie Oxley

Helleborus argutifolius Viv.

Family: Ranunculaceae

The genus name *Helleborus* comes from the Greek words *helein* meaning to injure, a reference to its toxic nature, and *bora* meaning food, thus 'poisonous food'. Care should be taken when handling all parts of this plant as it is both poisonous and an irritant, with roots being particularly toxic. Gardeners are advised to wear gloves when working with the plant.

In 1813 the name *Helleborus corsicus* was given to the plant illustrated, but in 1824 it was renamed *Helleborus argutifolius*. There is evidence, including a description and other material, to support the plant's identity as *H. argutifolius*, which is now recognized as the accepted name. The plant is an evergreen perennial with leaves on its flowering stem. It grows wild in Sardinia and Corsica and can be found in a number of different habitats, particularly in Corsica where it grows in woodland, on hillsides and in coastal regions.

H. argutifolius was identified by the Italian Domenico Viviani, Professor of Botany at the University of Genoa. Viviani founded a botanical garden at the university in 1803 and he occasionally received new plants from Stefano Serafino, a pharmacist from Bonifacio, Corsica, who collected across the islands of Corsica and Sardinia. Serafino had been Viviani's student and the specimens he sent were contributions to Viviani's floras of Corsica and Sardinia. In 1937 a revision of the plants he described was undertaken, but tragically, during the Second World War, his herbarium at the University of Genoa was destroyed. Some specimens that had previously been sent to other herbaria did survive.

H. argutifolius is an attractive plant which adds interest to the garden all year round, flowering during the winter months in Britain. It is a useful source of nectar for honeybees, solitary bees and bumblebees. The strong and attractive leathery blue-green leaves are divided into three leaflets which are sharply serrated. The word *argutifolius* means having sharp-toothed leaves and it is sometimes called the holly-leaved hellebore. The numerous pale green flowers, which together form a dome, are cup-shaped and consist of five perianth segments. These segments, known as tepals, act as both sepals and petals; they are not true petals and they do not fall from the flower after pollination. The nectaries lie in a ring inside the tepals. After pollination the nectaries and stamens fall, leaving the carpels protected by the remaining tepals. The carpels swell and split when the seeds are ripe. The seeds are released and carried away by ants attracted to sugars and fats in the elaiosome, a fleshy structure which is attached to the seed.

H. argutifolius is a larger plant than other hellebores and tolerates some shade; it grows well in organic, well-drained, limey soil, but it does not do well in heavy clay. Although it appears to be a strong and stout plant, it tends to fall outwards during the winter months and if conditions are harsh it may need staking. Later, old stems can be cut back to ground level. *H. argutifolius* can be used as a cut flower.

Helleborus argutifolius
Artist: Susan Christopher-Coulson
Coloured pencil
Accepted to the Archive 2004

S·M·C·C
MAR·04

Helleborus niger L.
Helleborus × *sternii* Turrill
Helleborus foetidus L.

Family: Ranunculaceae

Hellebores are found growing wild in western Europe from central Germany to southern Italy, across western Asia and in northern Morocco where they grow in mountainous regions, in woodland and in scrub. They are also found in China.

H. niger was named by Linnaeus in 1753 in *Species Plantarum*, and is commonly known as the Christmas rose. Sometimes it is referred to as the black hellebore due to the colour of its roots, the specific epithet *niger* meaning black. It grows in the Alps and Apennine Mountains in forest edges and on mountain slopes. *H. niger* is an evergreen perennial plant with large, deeply lobed, leathery leaves which are divided into seven, eight or nine segments. The leaves are usually taller than the flowers. The large white flowers appear singly on short stems in the middle of winter. Sometimes the flowers are tinged with pink or green. In a garden situation it prefers limey, humus-rich soil. This plant has received the Royal Horticultural Society's Award of Garden Merit.

H. × *sternii* is a hybrid between *H. argutifolius* and *H. lividus*. The features that *H.* × *sternii* display depend on how much of each parent is represented. *H. argutifolius* is a strong tall plant with green flowers, whereas the smaller and more tender *H. lividus* has markedly veined leaves and pinkish flowers. The original hybrid *H.* × *sternii* was first exhibited at the Royal Horticultural Society by T. Hilling & Co. of Chobham, Surrey in 1947. Two years later the hybrid was exhibited by Frederick Claude Stern, and named after him. Nurserymen have continued to improve *H.* × *sternii* by developing reliable cultivars. Stern was a botanist and horticulturalist who created a garden at Highdown, London where he developed several cultivars. He worked with Reginald Farrer and helped to finance a plant-collecting expedition to Yunnan and Kansu undertaken by Reginald Farrer and William Purdon. Stern was awarded the Victoria Medal of Honour by the Royal Horticultural Society and became Vice-President of the Society in 1962. He was Vice-President of the Linnaean Society from 1941 to 1958 and in 1956 he was knighted for his services to horticulture.

H. foetidus was named by Linnaeus in 1753 in *Species Plantarum*. It can be found growing wild in Britain and is generally known as the stinking hellebore. *H. foetidus* is an evergreen perennial plant. It has dark green leaves and clusters of light green, nodding, bell-shaped flowers, tinged with a purple edge, which appear in the late winter on thick succulent stems. The plant grows in shaded areas where it is unable to utilize the sun to heat the flowers and attract insects. However, the nectar produced by the many nectaries within the flower contain a yeast which raises the temperature within the flower cup, causing 'floral warming'. It is thought this may attract early pollinators such as bees. This plant has been given the Royal Horticultural Society's Award of Garden Merit.

Helleborus niger
Artist: Rosalind Timperley
Graphite pencil and watercolour
Accepted to the Archive 2005

Helleborus × sternii
Artist: Sheila Stancill
Graphite pencil and watercolour
Accepted to the Archive 2011

Helleborus foetidus
Artist: Barbara Munro
Watercolour and graphite
Accepted to the Archive 2014

Hesperantha coccinea (Blackh. & Harv.) Goldblatt & J.C. Manning

Family: Iridaceae

In 1864 *Schizostylis coccinea*, a South African plant, was described by William Curtis in *The Botanical Magazine* alongside a drawing executed by Walter Hood Fitch. However, in 1996 the plant was renamed *Hesperantha coccinea* in a paper by Peter Goldblatt, Curator of African Botany at Missouri Botanical Garden, and John Manning of the National Botanical Institute, Claremont, South Africa. The main reason for the transfer was the botanical similarity between the two genera; with the exception that in the wild the flowers of *Schizostylis* were red and they were found growing from rhizomes in damp places, whereas most species of *Hesperantha* had white or pink flowers and grew from corms in dry places. *Hesperantha coccinea* grows from a short rhizome in damp waterlogged areas and is found by streams, riverbanks and on the edge of marshland. Goldblatt and Manning suggested that over time the rhizome had developed from a corm to cope better with waterlogged ground. The observations of Goldblatt and Manning have since been supported by DNA analysis.

Schizostylis coccinea was originally discovered in the early nineteenth century and described by two Quakers, James Backhouse and William Henry Harvey. Backhouse was a nurseryman from York and embarked on missionary expeditions to Australia and South Africa where he botanized around Cape Town. Occasionally he was accompanied by Harvey. He returned to England and published his experiences in a book in 1844 called *A Narrative of a Visit to the Mauritius and South Africa*. Harvey was born in Ireland in 1811 and grew up in the countryside. He became an experienced and knowledgeable naturalist, well known for his studies of algae. After his father's death in 1834 he was keen to travel and in 1835 he went to South Africa as assistant to his brother Joseph, who was taking up an appointment as Colonial Treasurer in Cape Town. After his brother's early death, William took over Joseph's colonial duties and stayed in South Africa for another three years. After returning home, he published *The Genera of South African Plants*. In 1844 he became Curator of the Herbarium at Trinity College, Dublin and was appointed to the Chair of Botany in 1856.

Hesperantha means evening flower and *coccinea* describes its bright red colour. In South Africa it is known as the scarlet river lily. The narrow mid-green leaves are grass-like. The flowering spike can carry from four to fourteen flowers which face outwards and open up on one side. Each flower has six petals and is cup-shaped. The style is divided into three parts which gives rise to the original name *Schizo* meaning divided and *stylis* referring to the style. The flowers are pollinated by butterflies and long-tongued flies.

The plant is widely grown in gardens in Britain, its popularity unaffected by the change in name even though, as the botanist Dr Ken Thompson remarked in the gardening column of *The Daily Telegraph* newspaper, 'just when you've learnt how to spell the name of a plant, they change it!'

Hesperantha coccinea
Artist: Judyth Pickles
Graphite pencil and watercolour
Accepted to the Archive 2006

Hibbertia scandens (Willd.) Gilg

Family: Dilleniaceae

Hibbertia scandens is a plant native to New South Wales and Queensland. It was collected by Joseph Banks and Daniel Solander at Botany Bay in New South Wales in May 1770; it was also found at Bustard Bay in Queensland. The plants were taken on board the HMS *Endeavour* commanded by Lieutenant James Cook on his first voyage of discovery which had begun in 1768. Sydney Parkinson, the botanical artist on the voyage, made detailed drawings and colour notes of the plants, but he was not able to complete all the drawings as he died of dysentery during the journey home. On his return to England, Banks employed a number of artists to convert the drawings into watercolour paintings; one of these artists was Frederick Polydore Nodder. In 1778 Nodder made a watercolour illustration of *H. scandens* from the pencil drawing Parkinson had made at Botany Bay. An engraver, Daniel Mackenzie, was employed by Banks to prepare a copperplate engraving of the plant based on Nodder's watercolour painting. Unfortunately, the proposed *Florilegium* of plants collected on the voyage did not materialize at that time. Over two hundred years later the original engraved plates were found at the British Museum and *H. scandens* became one of 743 drawings to be published by Alecto Historical Editions in *Banks' Florilegium*, a project which started in 1980 and took ten years to complete.

Originally, the plant was given the name *Dillenia humilis* by James Donn, who was a protégé of Joseph Banks and Curator of the Cambridge Botanic Garden, but it was not fully described. In 1797, an English botanist and artist, Henry Cranke Andrews, published an illustration of the plant in *The Botanist's Repository, for New, and Rare Plants*. Andrews named the new plant collected by Banks as *Hibbertia volubilis*, after his friend George Hibbert, a wealthy merchant who funded various botanical expeditions. Hibbert was also a respected botanist and was elected a Fellow of the Royal Society and the Linnaean Society. In 1799 the plant was formally described and given the name *Dillenia scandens* by Carl Ludwig Willdenow, a German botanist and taxonomist. The specific epithet *scandens* refers to the climbing habit of the plant.

In 1806, a Swedish botanist, Jonas Carlsson Dryander, transferred the species into the genus *Hibbertia*. Dryander had been a pupil of Carl Linnaeus at Uppsala University. He arrived in London in 1777 and quickly made the acquaintance of Joseph Banks. He catalogued Banks's collections and became the Librarian of the Royal Society and Vice-President of the Linnaean Society of London. In 1893 the plant was renamed again by Ernest Friedrich Gilg as *Hibbertia scandens*. Gilg was the Curator of the Botanical Museum in Berlin. He published a catalogue of botanical families in collaboration with the botanist Heinrich Gustav Adolf Engler who was Professor of Botany at the University of Berlin.

H. scandens is a climbing or sprawling evergreen plant which has simple, glossy green leaves and solitary golden-yellow, five-petalled saucer-shaped flowers which are pollinated by beetles and bees. The plant's common names include snake vine and golden guinea vine.

Hibbertia scandens
Artist: Valerie Oxley
Graphite pencil, watercolour and coloured pencil
Accepted to the Archive 2003

Valerie Oxley

Hibiscus rosa-sinensis L.

Family: Malvaceae

Hibiscus rosa-sinensis is known as the Chinese hibiscus or rose of China. The genus name *Hibiscus* is from the Greek *hibiskos*, meaning mallow. The plant was described in 1753 by Linnaeus in *Species Plantarum*. Hibiscus plants are native to India, but have been introduced to areas around the equator including Mauritius, Madagascar, Hawaii, Fiji and China. *H. rosa-sinensis* was originally found growing wild in India, even though its specific Latin name means China-rose. It may have arrived in China in the twelfth century transported by traders. The exact location where it was originally found in the wild is not known.

H. rosa-sinensis was drawn by Sydney Parkinson in 1769 whilst he was on the *Endeavour* voyage with Joseph Banks and Daniel Solander. The plant was collected whilst the ship was anchored off Tahiti and the original specimen is in the herbarium at the Natural History Museum, London. *H. rosa-sinensis* was formally declared as Malaysia's national flower in 1960, overcoming competition from other flowers including the rose, lotus, magnolia and medlar.

H. rosa-sinensis is an ornamental plant, a perennial evergreen shrub with light grey, smooth bark. The simple ovate leaves are glossy green and are arranged in a spiral around the woody stems. The flowers are large and showy with a range of colours from white to pink through to red, orange, purple and peach. A white variety can be found in Hawaii. The solitary, trumpet-shaped flowers, which only last one or two days, appear in the axils of the leaves. The flowers have five petals united at the base. Beneath the petals are five joined sepals which form the calyx and below this is an epicalyx with sepal-like bracts. The filaments of the numerous stamens are joined into a red cylindrical structure around the style. The long style has five stigmas and the ovary is superior with numerous ovules. The fruit is a five-celled capsule which splits open when dry to release the seeds. In its native habitat the flowers are pollinated by insects, birds and butterflies.

H. rosa-sinensis is frost-tender in Britain but can be grown in a warm greenhouse or conservatory where there is bright light and good ventilation. The plants can be lightly pruned into shape, but generally require little pruning. *H. rosa-sinensis* can be grown outside during the summer months and brought indoors when the temperature drops. In some parts of the US it is grown as a hedge and the flowers are pollinated by hummingbirds.

Notable botanical illustrations of hibiscus were produced in the eighteenth and nineteenth centuries by botanical artists such as Pierre-Joseph Redouté and Pancrace Bessa.

Hibiscus rosa-sinensis
Artist: Pamela Furniss
Graphite pencil and watercolour
Accepted to the Archive 2007

X 4
X3
X 3
X4

Humulus lupulus 'Aureus'

Family: Cannabaceae

Humulus lupulus 'Aureus' is known as the golden hop and is a perennial plant. It is a colourful garden cultivar in the family Cannabaceae, the hemp family.

The original wild plant *H. lupulus* was identified by Linnaeus in *Species Plantarum* in 1753. Its native range is from Europe to Siberia and from northern Iran to Morocco. Early references to hop cultivation are from the seventh and ninth centuries, when hops were grown in monastery gardens in Germany and France. Sometimes dues were paid in hops. Hops have been found in excavations in York from before and after the arrival of the Vikings. The first records of hops being used in beer are generally thought to be from Germany. They were also grown in the Netherlands and it is probably from there that hops for cultivation arrived in England. The peak for brewing with hops was in the nineteenth century. Hops give beer its bitter taste and smell and they can act as a preservative in the brewing process. The plants start to grow in April and flower in July; the whole plant is cut down during harvesting, which usually takes place in August or September. The rootstock remains in the ground and can live for over twenty years. Hops were successfully grown in north Nottinghamshire in the seventeenth century, where they were known as North Clay hops. Problems with wilt destroyed the hops and the trade gradually declined. Plants which have escaped from cultivation in England can be found growing wild in hedgerows and scrubland areas.

H. lupulus is known as a bine plant. It has strong rough stems with stiff hairs which help the plant to climb; the stems twine around each other clockwise to help the plant to gain height, whereas plants that are described as vines use tendrils or suckers to gain height. The palmate leaves, with toothed margins, are opposite each other on the stem. The petalless flowers emerge from the axils of the leaves with male and female flowers on separate plants. The male flowers are in branched panicles with five sepals joined at the base and five stamens. The female flowers, which are used for brewing, are in spikes. They develop a papery cone-like structure with overlapping bracts. The bracts are clustered together in dense heads known as hops, which can be dried and used as decoration. The flowers are wind-pollinated, slightly scented and are attractive to butterflies. In the autumn the plant dies back leaving the rhizome to overwinter. The plant sends up vigorous new shoots the following spring.

H. lupulus 'Aureus' is a rapidly growing climber, with beautiful golden lobed leaves and attractive hops in the autumn. As a garden ornamental *H. lupulus* 'Aureus' can be grown as a decorative screen over a fence, on wires or on a trellis. The leaves of the golden hop appear more golden if they are planted in the sun. *H. lupulus* 'Aureus' has been given the Royal Horticultural Society's Award of Garden Merit.

Humulus lupulus 'Aureus'
Artist: Judyth Pickles
Graphite pencil and watercolour
Accepted to the Archive 2005

Hydrangea macrophylla 'Mariesii Perfecta'

Family: Hydrangeaceae

Hydrangea macrophylla is in the family Hydrangeaceae, which contains a number of sturdy and vigorous plants and shrubs. Its native habitat is south-central Japan but it can also be found as a naturalized plant in a number of countries including China, New Zealand and North and South America. The name hydrangea derives from two words, *hydro* meaning water and *angeion* meaning a vessel. The 'vessel' is supposed to refer to the shape of the seed capsule. However, it could be that the plant is named after the mythical character Hydra, meaning many heads, referring to the appearance of the fruit. The specific epithet *macrophylla* is from the Greek, *makros* meaning large and *phyllon* meaning leaf.

A Swedish naturalist and apostle of Carl Linnaeus, Carl Peter Thunberg, named and described the plant in 1784 in *Flora Japonica*. He called the plant *Viburnum macrophyllum*. Thunberg travelled to Japan in 1775 to work as a surgeon for the Dutch East India Company. Although travel within the country was closed to foreigners, he gained the respect of the local people and was able to make day excursions in the vicinity of Nagasaki where he collected plants. The plant was renamed *H. macrophylla* by Nicholas Charles Seringe in *Prodomus Systematis Naturalis Regni Vegetabilis*, published by Augustin Pyramus de Candolle in 1830. Seringe was a French botanist who studied medicine in Paris and served in the military. On leaving the army he studied in Bern where he became interested in botany and worked as a plant collector. In 1830 he was appointed Professor of Botany and Director of the Jardin des Plantes de Lyon.

The first hydrangea was introduced to Britain by the Quaker botanist Peter Collinson in 1736. It was grown from seed sent to Collinson from Pennsylvania. In 1753 Linnaeus named this plant *H. aborescens*. In 1789 Joseph Banks arranged for a new hydrangea to be shipped to Kew from China. This plant had its origins in Japan and was more colourful than Collinson's plants. In 1792 botanist James Edward Smith named this plant *H. hortensis*. In 1799 William Curtis wrote about the new hydrangeas in *The Botanical Magazine*, quoting Smith as saying that these new hydrangeas were 'magnificent and highly ornamental'.

Many hydrangeas found in gardens today have been successfully developed from *H. macrophylla*, including the cultivar *H. macrophylla* 'Mariesii Perfecta'. This is a woody, deciduous, flowering shrub, rounded in shape with an inflorescence described as a many-branched corymb. There are fertile flowers in the centre with five reduced petals and sepals, surrounded by an outer ring of larger sterile flowers. The flowers, which last from early summer to early winter, are visited by bumblebees, honeybees and hoverflies. The large, opposite dark green leaves have strongly ribbed branching veins and serrated margins. *H. macrophylla* 'Mariesii Perfecta' is a rewarding plant for the shrub border and it can also be grown in a container. It is susceptible to damage in harsh winters and early frosts. The flowers can be used as cut stems or dried for indoor winter arrangements.

Hydrangea macrophylla 'Mariesii Perfecta'
Artist: Pamela Furniss
Graphite pencil and watercolour
Accepted to the Archive 2011

A.
B
x2
C
x2
D
E
F
x3
G
x3
H
x10
J
x10

Iris reticulata M. Bieb.

Family: Iridaceae

Iris reticulata was first described by a German botanist, Friedrich August Marschall von Bieberstein, in 1808. *Iris* comes from the Greek name for a rainbow, probably referring to the many colour variations of the flowers. The specific epithet *reticulata* refers to the netting effect of the dead scale leaves covering the bulb. The plants can be found growing wild in the mountains of Russia, Turkey, Iran and Iraq.

Von Bieberstein had a military career and in 1793 he was posted to the Crimea where he was encouraged to pursue his interest in botany and natural history by another German naturalist, Peter Simon von Pallas. Von Pallas, who was Professor of Natural History at the Academy of Sciences in St Petersburg, was in the Crimea to collect specimens for the Academy. Von Bieberstein went on to collect specimens in the Caucasus and to explore the western shores of the Caspian Sea. He published an account of his travels, including descriptions of over seventy new plants. In 1799 he went to southern Russia to study silkworm production. This gave him an opportunity to study botany and to continue building his collection of plant specimens. Von Bieberstein married Maria Kristina Klick in 1804 and soon afterwards started to write *Flora Taurico-Caucasica* (1808–19). The work was published in two volumes, the first of which included a description of *I. reticulata*. The description of plants in the two books followed the Linnaean classification.

I. reticulata is a dwarf bulbous perennial growing to approximately 15cm high. The bulbs produce blue-green ridged leaves and erect flowers. The flowers are usually deep blue-violet, but there are variations. They have three fall tepals and three upright standard tepals. The fall tepals have yellow and white markings in the middle which act as bee guides and direct insects searching for pollen towards the centre of the flower. Three petaloid styles are found above each fall tepal, a stigma is situated under a flap on each one and a stamen lies under each style. When the bee enters the flower, attracted by the violet-like scent, it pushes between the fall petal and petaloid style and stigma. The stigmatic lip is forced open and pollen from another flower is brushed onto the receptive surface from the bee's back. As the bee backs out of the flower fresh pollen is deposited on its back from the single stamen and the stigmatic lip is forced to close as it passes. This enables the plant to avoid self-pollination. The inferior ovary is found at ground level.

I. reticulata can tolerate low temperatures if placed in a pot in a cold frame. Alternatively, it can be grown in an unheated greenhouse or planted directly into the soil. The bulbs cannot tolerate excess moisture as this causes them to rot. *I. reticulata* is an early-flowering bulb and appears in the spring, usually in February, at the same time as snowdrops. The plant is a popular spring garden ornamental, particularly suitable for rock and gravel gardens.

Iris reticulata
Artist: Jill Holcombe
Graphite pencil and watercolour
Accepted to the Archive 2004

Iris unguicularis Poir.

Family: Iridaceae

In 1783 René Louiche Desfontaines, a physician who studied botany in Paris, was elected to the prestigious French Academy of Sciences; this was a great honour for Desfontaines. Three years later he was appointed Professor of Botany at the Jardin des Plantes, and in 1793 became the first Chair of Botany at the Muséum national d'Histoire naturelle in Paris. Desfontaines spent ten years, from 1789 to 1799, in Tunisia and Algeria, studying the natural history of the area and collecting plants. On his return to France he published two volumes of *Flora Atlantica* describing the plants he found during his travels. He found a graceful iris which he named as *Iris stylosa*, the second part of the name referring to the iris's unusually long style. However, Desfontaines was not the first person to discover this plant. In 1785 another Frenchman, Jean Louis Marie Poiret, had been on a year-long expedition to Algeria sponsored by King Louis XVI; the aim of the journey was to compile a flora of the Barbary Coast. In 1789 Poiret published *Voyage en Barbarie*, which included the same iris that Desfontaines had found. He named the plant *Iris unguicularis*. The specific epithet refers to the narrow, claw-like end of the perianth segment. When Desfontaines discovered the plants were the same, he agreed to the convention that the older name, given by Poiret, should be used.

Poiret was a clergyman, botanist and explorer who was born in 1755 in St Quentin and died in 1834 in Paris. His first botany teacher was André Robert Forestier, a physician who lived in St Quentin. After the French Revolution Poiret became Professor of Natural History at the Central School in Aisne, where he trained researchers who continued his work by making further contributions to natural history.

I. unguicularis was introduced to Britain by the Hon. Rev. William Herbert, who also found the plant in Algeria. Similar species were also found in Crete, Greece, Syria and Asia Minor. Herbert was born at Highclere Castle, Hampshire in 1778. He was a son of the first Earl of Carnarvon and studied at Eton and Oxford. After an early political career Herbert was ordained and became Dean of Manchester. He was a writer on a wide range of subjects and a published poet. Herbert had always been interested in natural history and contributed illustrated articles on bulbous plants to *The Botanical Register* and *Curtis's Botanical Magazine*. The Herbert Medal was awarded in his honour by the International Bulb Society for advancing knowledge of ornamental bulbous plants. Herbert died in 1847. In 1869 Walter Hood Fitch illustrated *I. unguicularis* for *Curtis's Botanical Magazine* and there was an accompanying description of the plant by the editor, Joseph Dalton Hooker.

I. unguicularis, also known as the winter iris or Algerian iris, grows in rhizomatous clumps on poor soil. The evergreen leaves are long and strap-like; the flowers vary in colour from lavender blue to deep violet and are slightly scented. *I. unguicularis* brings welcome colour to the garden in the winter months, the flowers appearing in winter and early spring.

Iris unguicularis
Artist: Jill Holcombe
Graphite pencil and watercolour
Accepted to the Archive 2003

Leucojum vernum L.

Family: Amaryllidaceae

Leucojum vernum or the spring snowflake belongs to the family Amaryllidaceae. It was described by Carl Linnaeus in *Species Plantarum* in 1753. *Leucojum* is from the Greek *leukos* meaning white and *ion* meaning violet; the specific epithet *vernum* means spring. It is native to central Europe, ranging from Belgium to the Pyrenees, northern Italy, Bosnia and Herzegovina. It occurs on hillsides where the plant flowers as the snow melts.

L. vernum was listed in *A Garden of Pleasant Flowers* in 1629 and given the name *Leucoium bulbosum praecox maius* by the botanist and apothecary John Parkinson. The plant was described as a member of the family of *Leucoium bulbosum*, the bulbous violet. Parkinson gave it the name 'greater early bulbous violet'. William Curtis prepared and published a hand-coloured copperplate engraving of *L. vernum* for *The Botanical Magazine* in 1788, when he was Praefectus Horti of the Chelsea Physic Garden. *L. vernum* is now naturalized in some areas of Britain, having escaped from cultivation. It was first recorded in the wild in Dorset in 1866, and it has been recorded in Somerset.

L. vernum is a bulbous perennial which grows in a tuft. The flowers appear with two or more strap-like leaves which are fairly broad and glossy green. The leaves do not reach their full height until after the flowers have faded. The flowers have six equal perianth segments or tepals, which are not joined at the base and serve the dual function of petal and sepal. The tepals are white with a distinctive yellow or green spot near the tip. Plants from the western regions of the species tend to have a green spot on the tip of the petal, whereas the petal tips on plants from the eastern regions have a yellow spot. When the flower emerges from the protective spathe it hangs downwards on a slender pedicel. There are six stamens, each with yellow anthers and short white filaments; the ovary is inferior with three fused carpels. The flowers are an important source of nectar and pollen for visiting insects and bees in the early spring. *L. vernum* can be distinguished from the *L. aestivum*, the summer snowflake, by having one flower, occasionally two, per stem, instead of three to seven smaller flowers. The fruits contain whitish seeds which have an outgrowth on them called a strophiole which is attractive to ants. It is thought that the ants carry the seeds away to their underground nests and feed the fatty oils in the strophiole to their larvae. The seeds are not eaten and some are able to germinate.

L. vernum is cultivated as an ornamental bulbous plant. It is tolerant of waterlogged soils and can be found in damp woodland and river meadows. In British gardens it can be planted alongside streams and ponds in partial shade. The species has been awarded the Royal Horticultural Society's Award of Garden Merit.

Leucojum vernum
Artist: Neelam Modi
Graphite pencil and watercolour
Accepted to the Archive 2016

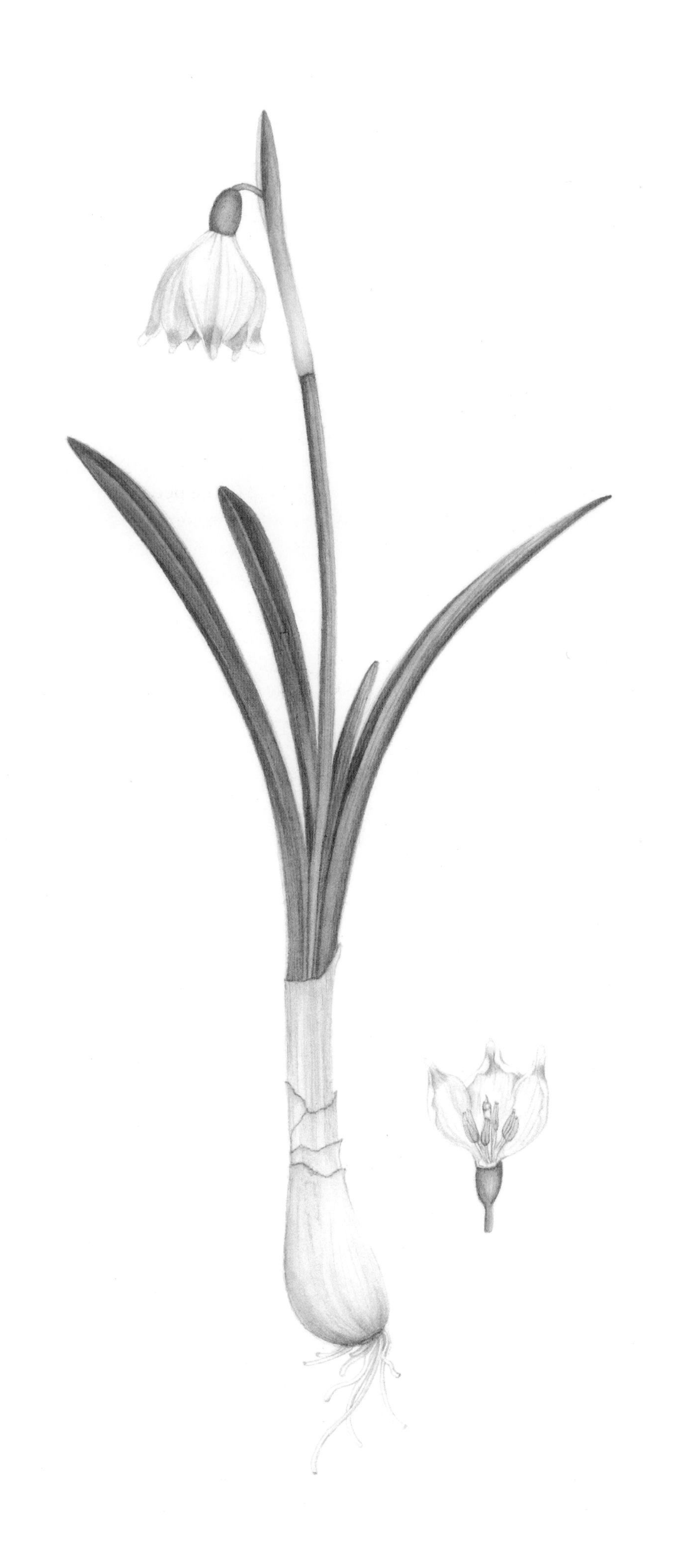

Leycesteria formosa Wall.

Family: Caprifoliaceae

Leycesteria formosa is commonly known as the Himalayan honeysuckle. It is native from the Himalayas to south-central China and Myanmar. It was described by Nathaniel Wallich, a Danish physician and botanist who went to India in 1807 as surgeon to the Danish Settlement at Serampore, West Bengal. In 1809 he became an assistant to William Roxburgh, a Scottish surgeon who was the East India Company's botanist in Calcutta. In 1817 Wallich became Superintendent of the Company's Botanic Garden in Calcutta, and in 1822 he travelled to Singapore to help establish a botanical garden at the request of his friend Sir Stamford Raffles. He continued to take part in expeditions around India, Singapore, Penang, Assam and the Cape until 1844. Wallich published two works, *Tentamen Florae Nepalensis* in two volumes and *Plantae Asiaticae Rariores* in three volumes. He was respected for the help he gave to plant hunters passing through Calcutta on their way to the Himalayas. He packed many of the specimens that were destined for England himself, and was particularly well known for packing seeds in brown sugar to protect them on their long sea voyage. The East India Company's Wallich Herbarium is held at the Royal Botanic Gardens, Kew. Roxburgh dedicated the genus *Wallichia* to him.

L. formosa was named after a friend of Wallich called William Leycester, who was Chief Justice of Bengal and a keen horticulturalist. The specific epithet *formosa* means beautiful. The plant was first described in 1824, in volume 2 of William Roxburgh's *Flora Indica or Descriptions of Indian Plants*. Wallich called the shrub 'charming'. The plant was also described in *Edwards's Botanical Register* in 1839, a botanical magazine that had been started in 1815 by Sydenham Edwards, a botanical illustrator. *L. formosa* was also collected by George Govan, Superintendent of the Saharanpur Botanical Gardens and by his successor, John Forbes Royle, who found it in Nepal. Royle sent seed to London and it was grown in the Horticultural Society's garden. The Society described the plant as able to survive through the winter without protection, but noted it had inelegant growth and dull green leaves. The plant was also described as 'not as handsome as anticipated', and it was generally regarded as 'disappointing'. In Australia and New Zealand, it is now considered an invasive species.

L. formosa is a deciduous shrub with hollow, green, upright stems, which are replaced by new growth from the roots every few years, or if affected by a hard frost. The leaves are pointed with wavy margins; they are opposite on the stem. The white flowers appear on new growth from pendulous racemes surrounded by a purple bract. Bees pollinate the flowers and the fruit is a purple black berry. *L. formosa* was grown on large estates as ground cover for nesting pheasants; the birds enjoyed eating the fruits. Despite the earlier comments it became a popular plant for Victorian shrubberies.

Leycesteria formosa
Artist: Pamela Furniss
Graphite pencil and watercolour
Accepted to the Archive 2007

×3
×2
×3
×4

Magnolia acuminata (L.) L.
Magnolia liliiflora 'Nigra' (G. Nicholson) Geerinck
Magnolia stellata (Siebold & Zucc.) Maxim.

Family: Magnoliaceae

The story of the magnolia starts in 1651 when Philip IV of Spain published the first known record of a magnolia, now known as *Magnolia dealbata*. The plant, which is very rare in the wild, had been discovered by Francisco Hernández de Toledo, a naturalist, explorer and private physician to Philip IV's grandfather, Philip II of Spain. Hernández sometimes used Mexican native names when recording the plants that he found.

In 1688 a magnolia was introduced to Britain from Virginia in North America by a missionary called John Bannister, who was working for the Bishop of London, Henry Compton. The Bishop was a keen gardener with a particular interest in trees. He sent missionaries to the Americas to collect plants for his garden at the Bishop's Palace in Fulham. Bannister's magnolia became known as *M. virginiana*. However, it wasn't until 1703 that the genus name *Magnolia* was established by a French monk and botanist called Charles Plumier, who described a tree growing on the island of Martinique in *Nova Plantarum Americanarum Genera*. Plumier gave it the genus name *Magnolia* in honour of the French botanist Pierre Magnol. Magnol was a physician but spent much of his time studying botany. He introduced the idea of plants being in families and was considered a forerunner of the emerging interest in the classification of plants. Magnol became Professor of Botany and Director of the Royal Botanic Garden, Montpellier.

M. acuminata was discovered by John Bartrum on the east side of North America. It flowered in England in 1762 after being raised from seed by Peter Collinson. *M. acuminata* is a deciduous tree with large green leaves which are downy on the underside. It has inconspicuous, slightly fragrant, yellow-green flowers and is commonly known as the cucumber tree, due to the shape of the fruits.

M. liliiflora is native to China (Hubei, Yunnan, Hunan and Fujian). It was widely used as a temple and garden plant in China and Japan. The goblet-shaped flowers of *M. liliiflora* 'Nigra' are reddish-purple on the outside and pale pink inside. It is a deciduous compact shrub which flowers in early summer.

M. stellata is native to Japan, where it grows by the sides of streams and in boggy areas. It was introduced into Britain about 1877, probably by Charles Maries who was collecting for the Veitch Nurseries. It is a rounded compact shrub with white fragrant flowers and long narrow leaves. It has a larger number of tepals than other magnolias and is a popular ornamental garden plant.

Magnolia acuminata
Artist: Cathrine Allsopp
Graphite pencil and watercolour
Accepted to the Archive 2009

Magnolia liliiflora 'Nigra'
Artist: Louise Lane
Graphite pencil and watercolour
Accepted to the Archive 2019

Magnolia stellata
Artist: Vivienne Taylor
Graphite pencil and watercolour
Accepted to the Archive 2005

Magnolia sieboldii K. Koch
Magnolia sieboldii subsp. *sinensis* (Rehder & E.H. Wilson) Spongberg.
Magnolia × *loebneri* 'Leonard Messel'
Magnolia denudata Desr.

Family: Magnoliaceae

William Sherard was one of the first people to adopt the genus name *Magnolia*, after Charles Plumier established the name 'magnolia' in 1703. Sherard was an outstanding English botanist, influenced by Joseph Pitton de Tournefort, a pupil of Pierre Magnol. Linnaeus adopted the name *Magnolia* in 1735 in *Systema Naturae* and gave a description of the plant in *Species Plantarum* in 1753.

The winter buds of magnolias are covered with furry scales that protect the flowers which often open in the spring before the leaves emerge. The flowers are on the ends of the branches; they usually have six to nine tepals and numerous spirally arranged stamens and carpels. Magnolias are ancient primitive plants which evolved before pollinating winged insects such as bees. Instead, they are pollinated by wingless beetles which stumble about amongst the stamens looking for pollen to eat. Magnolias have simple alternate leaves and can be deciduous or evergreen trees or shrubs. The fruits are cone-shaped with the seeds embedded in the receptacle for protection. When the fruits ripen the carpel splits to expose the orange to red seeds which are attached to the carpel by a silken thread until they fall. The wood is a creamy colour and can be used for decorative purposes such as veneer.

M. sieboldii was named after Philipp Franz von Siebold, a German botanist who studied Japanese flora. It is native to China, Japan, Korea and Manchuria and is known as the Korean mountain magnolia. It is a small deciduous tree thought to have been introduced to Britain by the Veitch Nurseries. *M. sieboldii* flowers are white and open in early summer.

M. sieboldii subspecies *sinensis* is native to a small area of Sichuan Province, China. The flowers are white, fragrant and saucer-shaped. The fruits are pendulous with scarlet seeds. It was collected by Ernest Henry Wilson and introduced to the Arnold Arboretum in 1908. It was introduced to England in 1920 from the nursery of Léon Chenault at Orléans.

Magnolia × *loebneri* 'Leonard Messel' was bred by the Head Gardener, James Comber, at Nymans Gardens owned by Leonard Messel. The flowers are lilac-pink on the outside and paler within. The original hybrid between *M. kobus* and *M. stellata* was created by Max Löbner, who was the Head Gardener at Bonn Botanical Gardens. It first flowered in 1917.

M. denudata, the Yulan magnolia, is native to China. For hundreds of years it was planted in the gardens of Chinese Buddhist temples and in the grounds of the Emperor's palace. Joseph Banks introduced it to Britain in 1780. *M. denudata* is a medium to low tree with bud scales that are covered in grey hairs; it has fragrant cup-shaped white flowers.

Magnolia sieboldii
Artist: Sheila Stancill
Graphite pencil and watercolour
Accepted to the Archive 2008

Magnolia sieboldii subsp. *sinensis*
Artist: Sheila Stancill
Graphite pencil and watercolour
Accepted to the Archive 2011

Magnolia × *loebneri* 'Leonard Messel'
Artist: Sheila Stancill
Graphite pencil and watercolour
Accepted to the Archive 2012

Magnolia denudata
Artist: Sheila Stancill
Graphite pencil and watercolour
Accepted to the Archive 2011

Mandevilla [Sundaville Red] = 'Sunmandecrim' (PBR) (Sundaville Series)

Family: Apocynaceae

John Lindley described the genus *Mandevilla* in 1840. He named it after his friend, botanist Henry John Mandeville, who was Queen Victoria's British Minister in Buenos Aires, Argentina. Mandeville had already sent many interesting new plants to England from tropical woodlands in South America.

The seeds of *Mandevilla* were collected by gardener and botanist James (John) Tweedie who started his career as a landscape gardener. Early in his career he secured a position as foreman at Dalkeith Gardens before becoming Head Gardener at the Royal Botanic Garden, Edinburgh. Later he worked on landscaping a new garden at Castlehill in Scotland and also at the adjoining estate of Sundrum, before moving onto Blairquhan Castle. Tweedie gathered a vast knowledge of plants by working in these gardens and harboured a desire to visit South America after hearing about the wonderful plants being discovered. An opportunity arose and in 1825 he travelled to Buenos Aires. It was there that in 1832 Tweedie met Charles Darwin and provided him with information about the area that Darwin was hoping to explore. Tweedie himself took part in several collecting adventures, resulting in the accumulation of a large collection of seeds, some of which he sent to William Dalton Hooker in Glasgow.

Seed of *Mandevilla* was sent to William Thomas Horner Fox Strangways, who was a foreign diplomat and important plant collector at Abbotsbury, Dorset. Strangways had introduced a number of new species into cultivation. The garden at Abbotsbury was expanded and the numbers of tropical and sub-tropical plants were increased; some plants were able to survive outdoors in the mild southern Dorset climate. Strangways presented seeds of *Mandevilla* to the Horticultural Society.

Mandevilla's native range is from Mexico to tropical America. It can be a bushy or climbing plant with tuberous roots. Stems of the climbing plants curl clockwise around a support, a typical feature of the Apocynaceae, the dogbane family. Evergreen leaves are simple and opposite and large trumpet-shaped flowers appear on the previous year's new growth. There are one to ten flowers on a raceme and these flowers usually have five green sepals and five coloured petals. Pollination in its native habitat is by bumblebees, hawkmoths and hummingbirds which collect the nectar. *Mandevilla* has two free carpels which develop into a double follicle in the form of two long pods, which dry and dehisce (burst open) lengthwise, expelling the seeds. The seeds are small and elongated, with long branched hairs at one end to enable wind dispersal.

The horticultural name of the cultivar illustrated is *Mandevilla* [Sundaville Red] = 'Sunmandecrim' (PBR) (Sundaville Series). Its common name is rock-trumpet. The database of the International Union for the Protection of New Varieties of Plants (UPOV) gives the breeders as Yasuyuki Murakami and Tomoya Misato. It is an ideal conservatory plant and flowers in late summer. It grows in the pavilions at Sheffield Botanical Gardens.

Mandevilla [Sundaville Red] = 'Sunmandecrim' (PBR) (Sundaville Series)
Artist: Mary Morton
Graphite pencil and watercolour
Accepted to the Archive 2013

Morus nigra L.

Family: Moraceae

The black mulberry *Morus nigra* is a deciduous fruiting tree. Its origins are not entirely clear, as there is often confusion with the white mulberry, *Morus alba*. Unfortunately, early distinctions were not established between the two plants. It is generally understood that the black mulberry was originally found in Persia. It was cultivated as a fruit and also used medicinally by the Greeks and the Romans. The plant was first described by Pliny the Elder in his manuscript *Historia Naturalis*. Pliny was a respected author and scientist who wrote that 'the mulberry is the wisest of trees because the buds do not open until the worst of the cold weather has passed'. However, he was not referring to plants in England.

Reputedly, the oldest black mulberry tree in England is growing at Syon House on the banks of the River Thames in London. It is thought to have been introduced from Persia and is mentioned in 1548 in *Names of Herbs at Syon* by the physician and botanist William Turner, who laid out the Tudor garden there with Edward Seymour, Duke of Somerset. Although *M. nigra* was planted at Syon House and is mentioned in various records the existing tree may not be the original 1548 tree.

In 1607 James I decided to help develop the silk industry by producing silk cocoons in Britain. He ordered that orchards should be planted containing mulberry trees to raise silkworms. The caterpillars feed exclusively on mulberry leaves and silk from the cocoons provides the material for the silk trade. It was thought that *M. nigra* was preferred because it was more suited to the British climate than *M. alba*, which had been used successfully elsewhere. Pamphlets were distributed until 1655, containing woodcuts showing how to raise the silkworms. Unfortunately, the experiment failed because the silk spun from caterpillars eating *M. nigra* was inferior to and coarser than the silk produced by caterpillars feeding on *M. alba*. The idea of producing silk in Britain was abandoned and instead James tried raising silkworms in British territories overseas.

There are other mulberry trees at Syon House which are quite bushy and it has been suggested that they might be connected with the rhyme 'Here we go round the mulberry bush'. In 1842, James Orchard Halliwell, a collector of English nursery rhymes, published a version of the song. Records suggest that female prisoners in Wakefield may have sung the song as they exercised around a mulberry bush in the prison yard. Alternatively, the 'cold and frosty morning' could refer to the failure of some of the experiments with the silk trade, when mulberry trees were affected by early frosts.

M. nigra is a slow-growing tree which becomes gnarled and twisted as it develops. A distinguishing feature of the black mulberry is the unusual heart-shaped leaf, which is rough to the touch. The flowers are green and inconspicuous. Some plants have male and female flowers on the same plant and can self-pollinate; others have male and female flowers on different plants. The edible fruit ripens to nearly black.

Morus nigra leaves with flowers
Artist: Mary Acton
Graphite pencil and watercolour
Accepted to the Archive 2003

Morus nigra leaves with fruits
Artist: Mary Acton
Graphite pencil and watercolour
Accepted to the Archive 2004

Paeonia emodi Royle

Family: Paeoniaceae

Paeonia emodi was originally placed in the Ranunculaceae family but in 1830 Swedish naturalist Karl Asmund Rudolphi and German botanist Friedrich Gottlieb Bartling decided that peonies were distinct enough to place them in their own family, Paeoniaceae. The full extent of the native range of *P. emodi* is from east Afghanistan to China (south-west Xinjiang) and west Nepal.

The name peony is thought to derive from a Greek mythological figure Paeon. The specific epithet *emodi* refers to the Latin name for the Himalayas, *emodi montes*, where the plant grows wild. Paeon was a student of Asclepius, a god of medicine and son of Apollo, the god of healing. Paeon used the milky liquid from the peony's root to treat a wound Pluto had received in a fight with Hercules. Asclepius was so enraged at his student's success in outshining his tutor that he ordered he should be killed. When Pluto was informed of Paeon's fate he had him changed into a flower, a peony, in gratitude for his cure.

P. emodi was first recorded in 1831 in the East India Company's list of dried specimens of plants. The herbarium specimens were under the care of the Superintendent, Dr Nathaniel Wallich, who developed the Company's Botanic Garden at Calcutta. *P. emodi* was formally described and validated in 1834 by John Forbes Royle, a British physician and botanist. In 1823 Royle was appointed Superintendent of the Botanical Gardens in Saharanpur. He was interested in the natural history of the Himalayas and his position at Saharanpur gave him the opportunity to commission artists to illustrate the plants he discovered.

P. emodi, sometimes known as the Himalayan peony, is found growing in thickets on the lower slopes of the mountains. It is a clump-forming perennial with tall stems and large, glossy-green, deeply cut leaves. The upper surfaces of mature leaves have small hairs along the veins, but the lighter green undersides of the leaves are hairless. The stems are smooth and generally light green, but they can be flushed red. The beautiful terminal flowers are large and white, with five to ten petals; sometimes there are two, three or four flowers on a stem. The stamens are numerous and golden yellow. There is usually one carpel, but sometimes two, covered in yellow hairs. There are three to four sepals and three to six bracts beneath each flower. In the wild the flowers are pollinated by beetles, but they are also attractive to bees. The fruit is a follicle, which contains several roundish scarlet seeds that turn brown and then black as they ripen. The follicle dries as it matures and dehisces, expelling and dispersing the seeds as it splits open. Peonies are well known for their medicinal properties as well as being cultivated as ornamental plants.

Paeonia emodi
Artist: Mary Morton
Graphite pencil and watercolour
Accepted to the Archive 2019

Papaver (Oriental Group) 'Patty's Plum'

Family: Papaveraceae

Papaver orientale was first collected as seed by the botanist Joseph Pitton de Tournefort on an expedition to the Ottoman Empire in 1700. Accompanying him on the expedition were the botanist Andreas von Gundelsheimer and the botanical artist Claude Aubriet. A pen and ink drawing of *P. orientale* was made in the field by Aubriet in 1701.

P. orientale is a deep-rooted, ornamental perennial with toothed, bristly, grey-green leaves which grow in a mound from the base of the plant. The flowers are cup-shaped and are usually shades of red to orange, some petals having a black blotch at the base. *P. orientale* was introduced to Britain in 1714. The name was validated in 1753 by Carl Linnaeus in *Species Plantarum*. In 1788 another oriental poppy was introduced to Britain, *P. pseudo-orientale*, followed by a third, *P. bracteatum*, in 1817. These poppies became known as the 'Oriental Group'. There are a number of cultivars from crosses between these three species, including *P.* (Oriental Group) 'Patty's Plum'.

P. orientale was also identified by Friedrich August Marschall von Bieberstein who collected plants in the Caucasus in the late eighteenth and early nineteenth centuries. Bieberstein was a naturalist who joined the military and later worked as an aide-de-camp to Count Mikhail Kakhovsky, a senior Russian general. Kakhovsky sent Bieberstein to the Crimea where he met the naturalist Peter Simon von Pallas who encouraged him to pursue his original interest in collecting plants. Bieberstein collected many plants whilst he was travelling with the army and he published an account of his travels in French, German and then English. He went to the Caucasus several times. In 1804 he was able to study Tournefort's herbarium in Paris, which included specimens from the Caucasus. From 1808 until 1819 he published *Flora Taurico-Caucasica* in which he described *P. Orientale.*

P. (Oriental Group) 'Patty's Plum' is a cultivar that has an interesting history. It was found growing on a compost heap at Kingsdon Nursery Garden in Somerset by Sandra Pope, a volunteer working in the garden. The nursery belonged to Patricia Marrow who propagated the plant. Although it had been known in the early 1990s it only became available for sale to the public in 1999. The name 'Patty's Plum' is a combination of Marrow's first name, Patricia, followed by a description of the colour.

The unique plum colour of the flowers can be variable, with the deeper plum colours being very popular with gardeners and illustrators alike, although they can turn slightly brown with age. *P. orientale* 'Patty's Plum' has beautiful crushed satin-like petals with a dark blotch at the base. Bees, attracted to the blue-black pollen, pollinate the plant. The fruit is a capsule; when the seeds are ripe and the capsule is dry, flaps at the top of the capsule open and the seeds are shaken out by the wind.

Papaver (Oriental Group) 'Patty's Plum'
Artist: Sally Strawson
Graphite pencil and watercolour
Accepted to the Archive 2013

Phytolacca americana L.

Family: Phytolaccaceae

Phytolacca americana was recorded by Carl Linnaeus in *Species Plantarum* in 1753. It is a member of the pokeweed family Phytolaccaceae. Its native range is from east Canada to Mexico, but it has been introduced to a number of other regions around the world, including Europe and Asia. The scientific name comes from the Greek *phyton* meaning plant and *lacca* referring to the deep red-purple of the fruits.

P. americana is found in the wild growing in rich soil at the edges of woods, in thickets, on waste ground, alongside railway lines and by roadsides. It is generally regarded as invasive. It was used in Native American culture for medicinal and culinary purposes, and grown in Europe as an ornamental plant and for its red dye. The common name, pokeweed, is thought to come from the Native American word *poken* meaning bloody and could refer to the red juice that is produced when the berries are squashed. The plant is sometimes known as the red-ink plant.

P. americana is a tall, robust, upright shrub with large, dark green, lance-like leaves which give out a pungent smell when crushed. The small, green to white flowers have petal-like tepals arranged in the form of a raceme on pale pink pedicels. A variety of pollinating insects are attracted to the flowers. As they ripen the berries gradually turn from green to glossy purple-black before they fall. Although the fruits are eaten by birds and some small mammals, the plant is poisonous if ingested by livestock and human beings. The seeds, spread by birds, can remain viable in the soil for a number of years.

Pokeweed grows from a central, tuber-like taproot, which can enlarge over several years. The emerging pinkish-red stems are hollow and readily produce red-stemmed branches which can grow to make a very large plant. In the autumn the stems turn to a deep magenta colour. Depending on its location *P. americana* can grow to over 2.5 metres in height during the summer months. In the winter the plant dies back to its taproot.

A beautiful red dye can be extracted from pokeweed berries which can be used for dyeing wool. The dye is fugitive and will fade in time unless a mordant is used to fix the colour. If the correct recipe is not used the colours can be disappointing, resulting in muddy creams and yellows. Pokeweed juice has also been used as writing ink. It is reputed that American soldiers used pokeweed ink to write letters home during the American Civil War. Surviving samples show the colour of the juice turned brown with age. Because of early accounts that the plant was used for medicinal purposes, research is continuing to discover whether it can be used in treatment for cancer and other ailments.

Followers of James Knox Poke, the eleventh President of the US, thought that the pokeweed was named in his honour. His supporters would display cuttings of pokeweed in their lapels or around their necks as a tribute during his campaign.

Phytolacca americana
Artist: Sheila Stancill
Graphite pencil and watercolour
Accepted to the Archive 2010

1.
x3
2.
x3

Plumbago auriculata Lam.

Family: Plumbaginaceae

Plumbago auriculata is native in Mozambique and across South Africa. The word *plumbago* comes from the Latin *plumbum*, a reference to lead, and *agere* meaning to resemble. Pliny the Elder (23–79 CE) referred to the plant as a possible cure for lead poisoning, possibly due to the colour of the stains from the sap on the skin. The specific epithet a*uriculata* means ear-shaped and refers to the two rounded lobes at the base of the leaf. The common name for the plant is Cape leadwort. It was believed that a twig from the plant placed in the thatch of a hut would ward off lightning.

Jean Baptiste Lamarck was a French naturalist who studied medicine and botany after leaving the army in 1766. In 1788 he was appointed Chair of Botany at the Jardin des Plantes, where he described many plants, including plumbago, in *Encyclopédie méthodique, botanique* published in 1786. The Swedish botanist and physician Carl Peter Thunberg, an apostle of Carl Linnaeus, named the same plant *P. capensis* in 1794, before it was realized that Lamarck had already named the plant.

Carl Ludwig von Blume described *P. auriculata* in *Bijdragen tot de flora van Nederlandsch Indië* published in 1826. Blume studied medicine at the University of Leiden and then worked in the Dutch East Indies. He was later appointed Director of the State Herbarium in Leiden and was elected a member of the Royal Swedish Academy of Sciences in 1855. Blume spent a considerable amount of time exploring west and central Java. It is thought he studied and described many of the plants whilst in the field, so that the details would be ready for publication when he returned. He described plants from over 170 plant families.

P. auriculata is an ornamental garden shrub. It has long thin stems and is often grown as a climber. The glossy green leaves are arranged alternately along the stems. The flowers are elongated racemes at the ends of the branches, with individual flowers having five open petals at the top of a long narrow tube. Each flower is held in a long narrow ribbed calyx made up of five fused sepals covered with long-stalked sticky glands. The sticky hairs on the calyx entrap and kill small insects, including non-pollinating predators such as flea beetles, thrips and aphids. There are five stamens and a single style with five stigmas, which are like small elongated projections at the top of the style. The colour of the flowers can range from pale to deep blue-violet and they have a darker central vein on each petal. Pollination is by insects attracted to the nectar. The sticky hairs on the calyx become attached to passing animals and they effectively disperse the seed. In Britain *P. auriculata* is usually grown in a heated greenhouse or conservatory, but it can be grown outside in a frost-free area. At Sheffield Botanical Gardens it is grown in the pavilions.

Plumbago auriculata
Artist: Patsy Hirst
Graphite pencil and watercolour
Accepted to the Archive 2004

PAH

Primula bulleyana Forrest

Family: Primulaceae

In the wild *P. bulleyana* grows alongside streams and in marshy alpine meadows. The plants grow in Yunnan, China and were collected in 1906 by the Scottish plant collector George Forrest. He recorded seeing masses of the plants growing in moist meadows stretching as far as the eye could see.

P. bulleyana was named after Arthur Kilpin Bulley, who was a cotton trader in Liverpool and an enthusiastic amateur gardener. In 1898 Bulley bought forty-five acres of farmland in Little Neston for a family house and garden. It was the fashion at that time for wealthy landowners to employ plant collectors to look for unusual plants that they could grow in their gardens. The Director of the Royal Botanic Garden, Edinburgh, Sir Isaac Balfour, was so impressed with George Forrest's perseverance, character and appetite for travel in difficult terrain that he recommended him to Bulley.

Forrest was initially apprenticed to a chemist where he learned about the importance of plants in medicine. But after receiving a small inheritance, he saw an opportunity to travel. He went to Australia to seek his fortune in the gold rush of 1891. On his return he worked in the Herbarium at the Royal Botanic Garden, Edinburgh. In 1904 Bulley employed Forrest to work for him and he was sent to north-west Yunnan, China. Forrest was not only looking for plants for Bulley's garden but also for Bulley's new venture, which was on a more commercial scale, a garden nursery to grow plants and collect seeds. This business would become Bees' Seeds. Bulley was Forrest's first sponsor and Forrest named a primula, *P. bulleyana*, in his honour. Bulley also employed the plant collectors Frank Kingdon-Ward and Roland Edgar Cooper to collect seeds in South America, Africa and China. After Bulley's death his daughter bequeathed the garden, now known as Ness Botanic Gardens, to the University of Liverpool.

P. bulleyana is known as a candelabra primula, a semi-evergreen perennial and moisture-loving plant grown as a garden ornamental. Scarlet-orange flowers, that open from orange-red buds, appear in tiers around an erect stem, which can grow to about 50 centimetres high. The leaves, which are arranged in a basal rosette, are long and green and taper at the base, the tip of the leaf being slightly rounded. The fruit is a capsule and contains numerous dark-coloured seeds.

P. bulleyana was drawn by the botanical artist Lilian Snelling in 1924. She worked at the Royal Botanic Garden, Edinburgh as an illustrator from 1916 until 1921. She left to work at the Royal Botanic Gardens, Kew and became the principal artist and lithographer for *Curtis's Botanical Magazine*. She painted *P. bulleyana* for the magazine and, although it was some years after Forrest worked in the Herbarium at the Royal Botanic Garden, Edinburgh, it is likely that the illustration by Snelling is from a seed supplied by Forrest from his travels in China. *Primula bulleyana* thrives in the Water Garden at Sheffield Botanical Gardens.

Primula bulleyana
Artist: Rosalind Timperley
Graphite pencil and watercolour
Accepted to the Archive 2007

R. Timperley '01

Primula vulgaris Huds.

Family: Primulaceae

The primrose, *Primula vulgaris*, is a welcome early spring flower which can be found growing wild in a variety of habitats from the west of Europe to the west Caucasus and Lebanon. The common name, primrose, comes from the Latin *prima rosa* and refers to the plant's appearance as the first rose-like flower of the year. When naming the plant, Linnaeus used the specific epithet *acaulis*, which means 'without a flowering stem', as can be found in other primulas. Nine years afterwards William Hudson used the specific epithet *vulgaris* which means common or widespread.

Hudson was a botanist and an apothecary. He named *P. vulgaris* in *Flora Anglica* which followed the Linnaean system and was published in one volume in 1762. He was the Botanical Demonstrator at the Chelsea Physic Garden and a sub-librarian at the British Museum. In 1778 he published a new edition of *Flora Anglica* in two volumes. Hudson had intended to publish a *Fauna Britannica*, but a fire at his house destroyed a great number of his literary works, plus his collections of insects and plants. He was devastated and decided to retire.

The primrose was the favourite flower of Britain's Prime Minister Benjamin Disraeli (Lord Beaconsfield). Bunches of primroses were sent to him by Queen Victoria when he was in office. When he died on 19 April 1881 primroses were laid on his tomb in Westminster Abbey. The practice was continued and 19 April became known as Primrose Day. Two years after Disraeli's death the Primrose League was formed by Lord Randolph Churchill; it was an organization designed to spread Conservative principles after the party was defeated by Gladstone in the 1880 general election.

P. vulgaris enjoys damp dappled shade in open woodlands and can be found on railway banks, in meadows and under hedgerows throughout Britain. It grows from a short rhizome and a basal rosette of green leaves. The leaves are irregularly toothed and the surface is puckered. They are oblong in shape and have a rounded tip, narrow base and short stalk. The plant has single pale-yellow flowers on short woolly stems. Five notched lobes spread out from the top of the corolla tube. The base of the lobes is golden yellow marked with honey guides. The flowers are rich in nectar and pollinated by long-tongued bees and flies and they are a source of nectar for early-emerging brimstone butterflies. There are two types of flower, distinguished by the positions of the style and stamens: they are either 'pin-eyed' (having a long style and stamens attached half way along the corolla tube) or 'thrum-eyed' (having short styles and stamens attached to the top of the corolla tube). The fruit is a capsule which is short and sits snugly within the calyx. As the fruit matures and dries the stem bends over and the black seeds fall to the ground around the plant. The seeds are dispersed by ants which are attracted to sticky oil on the surface of the seed. They carry the seeds a short distance from the parent plant and once they have taken the oil, they leave the seed to germinate. *P. vulgaris* is a popular garden plant for shady areas.

Primula vulgaris
Artist: Judyth Pickles
Graphite pencil and watercolour
Accepted to the Archive 2007

PIN-EYED FLOWER
x 2
THRUM-EYED FLOWER
x 3
x 3
PIN-EYED FLOWER

Prunus serrula Franch.

Family: Rosaceae

P. serrula was described by Adrien René Franchet in 1890. Franchet was the Director of the Muséum national d'Histoire naturelle in Paris and an experienced taxonomist. He described a large number of plants from China and Japan collected by French Catholic missionaries. Eventually, Franchet became overwhelmed with the vast numbers of plants arriving from China, particularly those collected by Pierre Jean Marie Delavay, who sent Franchet over 200,000 prepared specimens of which over 1,500 were new species. Franchet was unable to cope with the extra demands on his time and he died in 1889 before some of the beautifully prepared specimens were opened. It was many years before some of the plants were described.

Ernest Henry Wilson introduced *P. serrula* to Britain in 1908. Its native range includes Tibet and south-central China. Wilson collected for the Veitch Nurseries, but after meeting Charles Sprague Sargent, an American botanist and founding Director of the Arnold Arboretum in Boston, he also collected for Sargent. Wilson's third and fourth expeditions to China were sponsored by Sargent, who edited three volumes of *Plantae Wilsonianae*, highlighting Wilson's introductions. After Sargent's death in 1927 Wilson became the Keeper of the Arnold Arboretum, but his tenure was cut short when he was killed in a motoring accident in 1930.

George Forrest found *P. serrula* growing in Yunnan in 1913 on his third expedition to China. Forrest collected extensively in Yunnan sponsored by Arthur Kilpin Bulley, who created Ness Gardens in Cheshire and was the founder of the company Bees' Seeds.

P. serrula is a small, deciduous, ornamental tree, commonly called the Tibetan cherry. It is noted for its rich, shiny, reddish-brown bark which peels away as the tree matures. Multi-stems can be cultivated by pruning at an early stage; they look particularly outstanding in winter when their smooth bark can be clearly seen. Creating a multi-stemmed tree involves removing the leading stem, which encourages the tree to produce branches from near to ground level. However, horticulturalists suggest that planting three saplings together may be a much quicker way to create the same effect. To maintain the glossy appearance of the bark, annual scrubbing or wiping is recommended to remove any grime on the surface.

P. serrula has simple, narrow, serrated leaves, arranged alternately along the branch. They are light green in the spring before turning golden yellow in the autumn. The white flowers usually appear on the branches just as the leaves emerge. They have five petals which form a small bowl shape and, although sometimes solitary, they usually appear in a cluster of two to four flowers. Pollination is by bees and other insects. The small, oval fruits are like cherries. The handsome specimen of *P. serrula* at Sheffield Botanical Gardens was grown as a single-stemmed upright tree as shown in the illustration.

Prunus serrula
Artist: Janice Relton
Graphite pencil and watercolour
Accepted to the Archive 2004

approx. 8 metres

Pterocarya fraxinifolia (Poir.) Spach

Family: Juglandaceae

Pterocarya fraxinifolia is in the walnut family. The name *Pterocarya* is derived from the Greek, *pteron* meaning wing and *karyon* nut. The specific epithet *fraxinifolia* refers to *fraxinus* meaning ash. *P. fraxinifolia* is native to an area which extends from the Caucasus to eastern Turkey and northern Iran. In Turkey it can be found in humid forests along the Black Sea coast.

P. fraxinifolia was discovered by a French botanist and plant collector, André Michaux, who introduced it to France in 1784. Michaux was born near Versailles in 1749 and spent three years studying and collecting plants in England, Spain and France. In 1782 the French government sent him to Iran to look for plants and cereal grains. His next plant-collecting expedition was to North America, where he collected forest plants in order to help restock forests near Paris. Unfortunately, most of his plants were lost during a shipwreck. He died from fever in Madagascar in 1802.

P. fraxinifolia was also found and identified by Karl Heinrich Emil Koch, a German botanist, who collected in the Caucasus and Turkey in the mid-nineteenth century. Koch worked at the Berlin Botanical Gardens and in 1852 he became General Secretary of the Berlin Horticultural Society. In 1859 he was appointed Professor of the Agricultural High School in Berlin. The tree was identified again by the French botanist Édouard Spach, who studied botany in Strasburg. He became Curator for Botany at the Muséum national d'Histoire naturelle in Paris and he contributed to the fourteen volumes of *Histoire naturelle des végétaux: phanérogames* and five volumes of *Illustrationes Plantarum Orientalium*.

P. fraxinifolia, known as the Caucasian wingnut, is a striking, large, deciduous tree which has male flowers in the form of thick catkins in the spring. The wind-pollinated female flowers are on longer and thinner catkins on the same tree. The fruits develop into green winged nutlets which turn brown in the autumn and hang from the tree like a string of beads. The pinnate, shiny-green leaves turn yellow in autumn. They are arranged alternately on the branch and have seven to twenty-one leaflets. In appearance the leaves are similar to those of the ash. *P. fraxinifolia* grows very quickly and is cultivated as an ornamental tree in Britain, mainly in large gardens or in parkland. It prefers wet or damp areas and is happy near riverbanks. In Iran it can be found on riverbanks along with willows and poplars. The trees tend to throw up suckers from their roots which appear around the base of the tree, giving them a luxuriant and bushy appearance. (Lime trees produce shoots from the base of the trunk, giving the same bushy effect.) *P. fraxinifolia* can have several stems or trunks which spread widely as they grow; occasionally the branches need supporting. As the tree ages the bark on the trunk turns from light to dark grey and becomes deeply grooved. *P. fraxinifolia* was introduced into Britain in about 1810. Notable specimens can be found in the Cambridge and Sheffield Botanical Gardens.

Pterocarya fraxinifolia
Artist: Pamela Furniss
Graphite pencil and watercolour
Accepted to the Archive 2004

C < 60cm
11-25 leaflets
B. Female < 20cm
B. Male < 14 cm
x 5
♂
B2
x 6
♀
B1.
A.
D < 60 cm.
Pterocarya
fraxinifolia
F.
E. < 20m

Quercus robur L.

Family: Fagaceae

Quercus robur, the English or pedunculate oak, is a slow-growing, much-loved British tree. It was described by the Swedish botanist Carl Linnaeus in *Species Plantarum* in 1753. *Q. robur* is found throughout most of Europe, Asia Minor, North Africa and the Caucasus. It is a large tree, often living more than 500 years. *Q. robur* was included in *Flora Rossica* written between 1784 and 1788 and published by Peter Simon von Pallas, a German naturalist who worked at the Russian Academy of Sciences in St Petersburg. The publication was compiled for Catherine II and was the first illustrated Russian flora. *Q. robur* was recorded because of its economic value.

Oak woodlands were once common in Britain and planted for the building of ships and the manufacture of furniture. The specific epithet *robur* means robust and this refers to the oak's robust and strong timber. Oak bark was used for tanning leather and men were employed to peel the bark from felled trees, the timber being used for fuel and producing charcoal. In the reign of Elizabeth I, a law was introduced to protect oaks from over-felling. Another British oak, *Quercus petraea*, known as the sessile oak, found on rocky ground in the north and west of Britain, can hybridize easily with the pedunculate oak. Where the distribution of the two oaks overlap, identification can cause confusion.

Q. robur is a large deciduous tree; the trunk is grey and darkens with age. The buds are alternately arranged, with some buds appearing together in a cluster at the tip of the twig. The deeply lobed green leaves have a short stalk and they have distinctive, rounded, ear-like auricles at the base of the leaves. The flowers emerge at the same time as the leaves. The male flowers hang in long green catkins, which produce copious amounts of yellow, wind-dispersed pollen. The female flowers are stalked and rounded; they are less conspicuous than the male flowers and have a cluster of feathery stigmas on top. The fruits are pedunculate nuts and consist of an enclosed seed inside a cup-like, scaly structure; they are commonly known as acorns. The fruit is green, turning to brown in the autumn. They are dislodged by wind and animals as they dry and dispersed by small mammals and birds.

Q. robur is host to a large number of galls. One of the most well known is the oak-apple gall, caused by a wasp called *Biorbiza pallida*. Oak Apple Day is traditionally celebrated on 29 May and commemorates the restoration of Charles II, who escaped from the Roundhead army by hiding in an oak tree. In the past anyone who failed to wear a sprig of oak leaves or oak apples on that day was thrashed with nettles. Variations of the custom are still celebrated in different parts of the country. Oak galls have been used to make black ink and acorns have been used for animal feed, particularly for pigs grazing in oak woodland. The right to pannage means that people are allowed to graze their livestock in oak woods, as in the New Forest, Hampshire.

Quercus robur
Artist: June Mary Huckerby
Graphite pencil and watercolour
Accepted to the Archive 2015

Rhododendron luteum Sweet

Family: Ericaceae

Rhododendron luteum, the honeysuckle azalea or the yellow azalea, is found from Poland to the Caucasus and Turkey. It is widely cultivated in Britain on acid soils as an ornamental plant. The genus name comes from the Greek, *rhodo* meaning rose and *dendron* meaning tree. The specific epithet *luteum* means yellow and refers to the colour of the flowers.

In 1700 Joseph Pitton de Tournefort, Professor of Botany at the Jardin du Roi in Paris, embarked on an expedition to the Levant on the instructions of King Louis XIV. Observations from this expedition were recorded in *Relation d'un voyage du Levant* posthumously published in 1717. Amongst the plants Tournefort recorded was *R. luteum* which he found in the hills of Pontus, northern Turkey. He had a drawing made and wrote a description naming the plant *Chamaerbododendron Pontica Maxima mespilifolia flore lutea*. However, he did not send plants or seeds to the Jardin du Roi in Paris. The botanical artist Claude Aubriet who accompanied Tournefort undertook all the drawing required during the twenty-seven-month expedition.

R. luteum was also found in the Crimea by Peter Simon von Pallas, a German naturalist. In 1792 Pallas sent seeds to Lee & Kennedy, nurserymen of Hammersmith, London. During an exchange of exotic plants *R. luteum* was sent from the Chelsea Physic Garden to the nursery garden of Thomas Watson in Islington where it was brought into flower. In 1826 a hand-coloured illustration of *R. luteum* by William Clark appeared in a publication by Richard Morris called *Flora Conspicua*. William Clark was draughtsman to the London Horticultural Society and illustrated many floras in the 1820s and 1830s. *R. luteum* was described by Robert Sweet in 1830. Sweet was a horticulturalist and botanist who trained as a gardener and worked at a number of famous London nurseries. He published several botanical books with illustrations drawn by Edwin Dalton Smith, a botanical artist who was working for the Royal Botanic Gardens, Kew.

R. luteum is an upright, deciduous, bushy, perennial shrub or small tree. Young twigs are usually red-brown and covered with bristly hairs. The leaves are alternate, flat and pointed with shallow teeth. They have sticky glandular hairs on the upper and lower surfaces and the margins of young leaves roll downwards. The flower buds are chestnut-brown and hairy. Fragrant, funnel-shaped, yellow flowers open in a cluster just as leaves are beginning to emerge. There is a dark yellow blotch on the upper corolla lobe and pollination is by bees and other insects. The fruits are dehiscent capsules and the seeds are dispersed by birds. The plant can also reproduce by suckering. In the autumn the leaves change from green through yellow, red and orange adding extra colour to shrubbery borders. *R. luteum* has escaped from cultivation and is considered invasive in some parts of the country. It inhibits woodland regeneration and is toxic to animals if ingested.

Rhododendron luteum
Artist: Sue Nicholls
Graphite pencil and watercolour
Accepted to the Archive 2005

Sarcococca confusa Sealy

Family: Buxaceae

Sheffield Botanical Gardens hold the National Collection of *Sarcococca* in the family Buxaceae. The common name for the plant is sweet box or Christmas box. In 1826 the genus was named *Sarcococca* by John Lindley and listed in *Edwards's Botanical Register*. The name *Sarcococca* is of Greek derivation and refers to the fleshy berry. *Sarcococca* is native to China.

A species of *Sarcococca* called *S. wallichii* was discovered in the wild by Nathaniel Wallich in 1821. In 1916 it was described by Otto Staph, an Austrian botanist and taxonomist. The first introduction of a *Sarcococca* to Britain was around 1825 by Joseph Dalton Hooker. It was named *S. hookeriana* var. *hookeriana*. Another species, *S. ruscifolia*, was found in China in 1887 by Augustine Henry. There were also introductions from China by Ernest Henry Wilson in the early twentieth century and by Charles Roy Lancaster, plantsman and gardener, during a plant-collecting expedition in Yunnan, China in 1980. *S. confusa* is native to Sichuan and Hubei provinces in China. In 1949 it was described by Joseph Robert Sealy in the *Journal of the Royal Horticultural Society*. Sealy started work with Thomas Archibald Sprague at the Royal Botanic Gardens, Kew in 1925 and became a specialist in plants from China. In 1927 he worked in the Herbarium at Kew with Arthur William Hill. Sealy married the botanist and botanical artist Stella Ross-Craig, who is well known for her drawings of British plants.

S. confusa is a slow-growing, dense evergreen shrub. It is fragrant with a scent like vanilla that wafts on the wind and can be enjoyed if the plant is near a path. The simple, alternate leaves are dark green and shiny; they have entire, slightly wavy edges. *S. confusa* has a variable number of male and female flowers on the same plant, which appear in the axils of the leaves. The flowers, in mixed clusters, appear from December to February with the male flowers above the female ones. The female flowers have between four and six sepals and two or three styles, and are pollinated by insects, including early bees in mild winters. The male flowers are more conspicuous, with four sepals and one to four stamens; the stamens have white filaments and cream anthers. The plant has a fibrous root system and green to purple shoots which are hairy in young plants. The plants can be propagated by semi-hardwood cuttings and will set seed successfully around the garden in moist shady areas. The fruit is a two- or three-celled drupe, which changes in colour from green through dark red to black as it matures. Two to three shiny black seeds are produced which are dispersed by birds and mice.

S. confusa is an ornamental plant, and sprigs in a vase with snowdrops look particularly attractive indoors. The artist has drawn the branching twigs with and without leaves to show their dense structure.

Sarcococca confusa
Artist: Sheila Stancill
Graphite pencil and watercolour
Accepted to the Archive 2016

0·85m
x8
x4
c.
x2
x2
c.
c.
a.
b.
e
x8
d.

Sequoiadendron giganteum (Lindl.) J. Buchholz

Family: Cupressaceae

William Lobb was one of the first plant collectors in the nineteenth century to be employed by the Veitch Nurseries based in Exeter, Devon. Lobb was a gardener and an enthusiastic amateur botanist who was keen to travel and collect previously unknown plants. In 1840 he was sent by James Veitch to South America and from 1849 he was collecting in North America.

In 1852 Augustus Dowd, who was hunting bears, discovered some giant trees in the foothills of the Sierra Nevada mountains, California. Branches from the trees were sent to Dr Albert Kellogg, a medical practitioner and botanist, one of the founders of the Californian Academy of Sciences. Kellogg delayed writing a description of the giant tree until he had received more plant material; he particularly wanted to see the flowers and fruits. Kellogg planned to call the tree *Washington gigantea* in honour of the first president of the US. Kellogg showed the branches to William Lobb, who had recently arrived from England. Lobb quickly made his way to the grove and collected seed and two small trees. He secretly returned to England with the plant material and shared some of it with John Lindley, Professor of Botany at the University of London. John Lindley prepared a description of the species and named the tree *Wellingtonia gigantea* in honour of the Duke of Wellington, who had defeated Napoleon at Waterloo. The use of the genus name *Wellingtonia* caused an uproar amongst American botanists, who were affronted that the world's largest tree had been named after an English duke by a botanist who had never seen it. In 1847 a Viennese botanist, Stephan Ladislaus Endlicher, assigned the trees to a new genus that he called *Sequoia*. In 1854 a French botanist, Joseph Decaisne, published a description of the tree, naming it as *Sequoia gigantea*. In a sequel to this story, it would appear that John Lindley knew about a packet of seeds that had arrived in Scotland in 1853, about four months earlier than those brought back by Lobb. The seeds were sent from John Matthews to his father Patrick Matthews, a Scottish laird and botanist. Father and son made a claim to be the first to name and introduce the tree to Britain.

In 1939, the tree was renamed *Sequoiadendron giganteum* by an American botanist, John Theodore Buchholz. Common names for the tree are wellingtonia, giant redwood or simply big tree. Sequoia trees are the largest in the world. The oldest has been recorded as 3,200 years using dendrochronology sampling.

S. giganteum is an evergreen tree, with awl-shaped leaves arranged spirally on shoots. The red-brown bark is fibrous and furrowed and is thought to protect the tree from fire damage. Male and female cones are found on the same tree. Pollen, which is carried by the wind, is released from the male cones situated on the tips of branches. Winged seeds develop in fertilized female cones; these have spirally arranged scales and can stay green and closed for up to twenty years. They open with heat or by insect damage and the seeds are released.

S. giganteum was introduced to the Cedar Lawn, now the Evolution Garden, at Sheffield Botanical Gardens in 1967.

Sequoiadendron giganteum
Artist: Julie Small
Graphite pencil
Accepted to the Archive 2005

x 2

Stachyurus praecox Siebold & Zucc.

Family: Stachyuraceae

The name *Stachyurus praecox* comes from Greek and Latin: the Greek *stachys* means an ear of grain and refers to the flower spike; the Latin *oura* means tail and refers to the twelve to eighteen florets which hang from the branch like tails. The specific epithet *praecox* is from the Latin, *prae* meaning before and *coxi* meaning ripening, referring to the early appearance of the flowers in spring. The plant is sometimes known as spike-tail.

S. praecox is from Japan and was discovered by the German physician Philipp Franz von Siebold, who studied medicine at the University of Würzburg. He was inspired by the naturalist, geographer and explorer Friedrich Wilhelm Heinrich Alexander von Humboldt after reading books about the latter's plant-collecting expeditions. Siebold was keen to travel and applied to become a surgeon on board the ship *Adriana*. During his voyages he stayed for a few weeks with the Governor General of the Dutch East India Company, to recover from an illness. He so impressed the Governor General, and also the Director of the Botanical Garden at Bogor, Indonesia, with his learning and scholarship, that they posted him to Japan. In 1823 he went as a physician and scientist to a small island called Dejima in Nagasaki Bay, a trading post of the Dutch East India Company. During his time in Japan, Siebold founded a medical school and the students helped him to find and collect plants from restricted areas. Siebold described the plants he had collected in *Flora Japonica*, a publication which was started in 1835. He was assisted by Joseph Gerhard Zuccarini, Professor of Botany at the University of Munich.

S. praecox is a deciduous ornamental shrub. When the shrub is young the bark is red and covered with white lenticels; the bark turns grey with age. The pendulous flower spikes appear in the axils of the leaves in the autumn and hang there until spring. The flowers open up on bare, rich brown branches in racemes of four-petalled, pale yellow, bell-shaped flowers. In natural populations there are plants with female flowers only as well as plants that are hermaphrodite. It is thought the hermaphrodite plants are still undergoing the process of evolution. In time they may become male-only plants as they don't appear to set fruit. The flowers are followed by the appearance of simple, mid-green leaves with serrated edges and long points. The leaves turn from green to yellow through orange to red in the autumn, making it an attractive shrub to enjoy later in the year as well as in the spring. Early foraging insects such as solitary bees and hoverflies pollinate the unscented flowers. The fruit, a four-chambered berry containing a number of seeds, turns from green to purple as it ripens.

In Japan the plant is known as a pioneer shrub as it is one of the first plants to grow in cleared areas. Its natural habitat is on moist, well-drained, acidic soil at forest edges.

Stachyurus praecox
Artist: Barbara Munro
Watercolour and graphite
Accepted to the Archive 2013

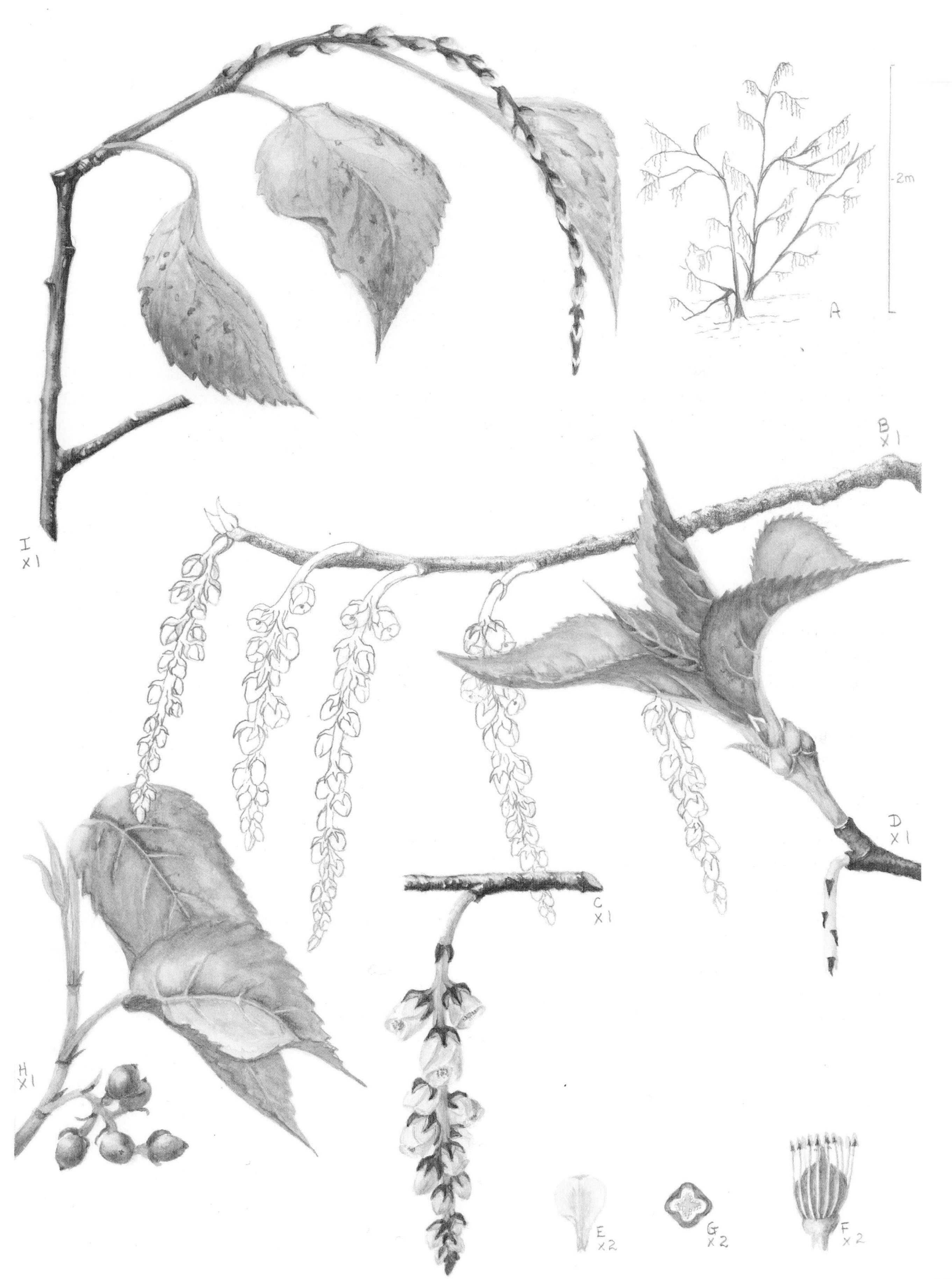
2m
A
B
x1
I
x1
C
x1
D
x1
H
x1
E
x2
G
x2
F
x2

Symphoricarpos albus (L.) S.F. Blake

Family: Caprifoliaceae

Symphoricarpos albus is in the Caprifoliaceae or honeysuckle family. Its native habitat is in subarctic America and the north and west-central states of the US, in dry to moist places in forest clearings and on rocky slopes. The name *Symphoricarpos albus* comes from *symphorein*, which means to bear together and *karpos* which means fruit. The specific epithet *albus* means white and refers to the colour of the fruit; it is known as the snowberry. One species of *Symphoricarpos* originates from central China and is called *S. sinensis*, the Chinese coralberry.

S. albus was first described by Carl Linnaeus as *Vaccinium album* in *Species Plantarum* in 1753. Linnaeus used a specimen from a collection made by Pehr Kalm, a Swedish explorer and botanist. Kalm travelled to the North American colonies for the Royal Swedish Academy of Sciences to collect seeds that might be useful in agriculture. In his description Linnaeus gave the habitat as Pennsylvania. However, Henry Knute Svenson, Curator of Brooklyn Botanic Garden, discovered, after studying correspondence from 1751 between Linnaeus and Kalm, that it was first found in Canada. The plant was described several times, but the accepted classification was undertaken by Sidney Fay Blake, an American botanist and taxonomist, who worked for the US Department of Agriculture.

In 1803 US President Thomas Jefferson commissioned Captain Meriwether Lewis and his friend Second Lieutenant William Clark to embark on an expedition to explore and map western North America and send back seeds of new plants. Lewis sent seeds and plant material to Bernard McMahon who was one of two selected nurserymen to grow the seeds and roots that Lewis and Clark collected. In 1812 McMahon sent some cuttings of *S. albus* to Jefferson. In 1813 Jefferson described the plant to Adrienne Catherine de Noailles, Comtesse de Tessé, as 'A very handsome little shrub the size of a currant bush. Its beauty is in the great production of berries through the winter, after the leaves have fallen. We call it the snowberry bush as no botanical name being yet given to it.'

S. albus is an ornamental plant used for ground and game cover which can spread by suckering and in some areas it has become naturalized. The opposite green leaves are usually rounded, but sometimes they have a few lobes. *S. albus* has small bell-shaped pink flowers which cluster at the ends of twigs. There are four or five sepals joined at the base and four or five petals, the inner sides of which are white and are usually covered with white hairs. Pollination is by bees. The white fruits weigh the twig downwards in a graceful arch. They are not generally eaten by birds and so remain on the shrub after the leaves have fallen in the autumn, making it an attractive plant for the winter garden. *S. albus* was introduced into Britain from North America in 1817.

Symphoricarpos albus
Artist: Eleni McLoughlin
Graphite pencil and pen and ink
Accepted to the Archive 2019

a x5
b x1.25
c
d
e
F

Veltheimia bracteata Harv. ex Baker

Family: Asparagaceae

In 1797 a hand-coloured engraving of *Veltheimia viridifolia* appeared in volume 1 of a publication called *Plantarum Rariorum Horti Caesarei Schönbrunnensis*, published by the Dutch scientist Nikolaus Joseph von Jacquin in four volumes which appeared between 1797 and 1804. The illustration is thought to have been painted by Johann Scharf and engraved by Franz Anton von Scheidel. Jacquin studied botany, chemistry and medicine at Leiden University. After moving to Vienna, he was instructed by Emperor Franz Stephan to go to Central America to collect plants for his gardens at the Schönbrunn Palace.

The naming of the genus *Veltheimia* is attributed to Johann Gottlieb Gleditsch who became Professor of Botany at the Collegium Medico-Chirurgicum in Berlin. Gleditsch was well known for his experiments showing the effect of climate change on plants and he was one of the first people to acknowledge the role of insects as pollinators. He named *Veltheimia* after a German patron of botany, August Ferdinand Graf von Veltheim. The original specific epithet *viridifolia* means green leaves and refers to the striking, glossy green leaves of the plant.

The plant was later renamed *V. bracteata* and described in 1897 by John Gilbert Baker, who was a botanist at the Royal Botanic Gardens, Kew from 1866 until 1899, and Keeper of the Herbarium from 1890 until 1899. Baker wrote handbooks about a number of plant families. He was elected a Fellow of the Royal Society and was awarded the Veitch Memorial Medal by the Royal Horticultural Society in 1907. *V. bracteata* was also described by William Henry Harvey, an Irish naturalist, who was a friend of Joseph Hooker. Harvey went to Cape Town where his brother was the Colonial Treasurer and became his assistant. He succeeded to the post on the death of his brother. Whilst still in office he prepared three volumes of *Flora Capensis*.

V. bracteata is also known as the forest lily or the winter red-hot poker. It can be found growing wild in clumps in moist areas in the forests and scrubby coastal regions of the eastern Cape of South Africa. It is a semi-deciduous, bulbous plant; sometimes the leaves die back during the non-flowering season. The leaves are long, strap-shaped and glossy with wavy edges and they form a rosette as they emerge from the top of the bulb. The buds are upright and can have a green tinge at the tip. The flowers appear in a dense, long raceme at the top of a straight stalk which is mottled with purple. The colour of the flowers varies and can range from light pink to orange-pink before eventually becoming a deep rose-pink colour. They are tubular and hang downwards when fully open. In favourable conditions the flowers can last for about four weeks. They have long thin concave bracts tapering to a point; the specific epithet *bracteata* means having bracts. They are pollinated by birds. Black seeds are held inside large three-winged papery capsules and are dispersed by wind. In Britain the plant can be successfully grown indoors.

Veltheimia bracteata
Artist: Elaine Shimwell
Coloured pencil
Accepted to the Archive 2005

Viburnum × *bodnantense* 'Dawn'

Family: Viburnaceae

Viburnum × *bodnantense* is a hybrid cross made initially in 1933 (at the Royal Botanic Garden, Edinburgh) between *V. farreri* (formerly *V. fragrans*) and *V. grandifolium*, using the latter as the maternal parent plant. *V. grandifolium* was collected in Bhutan in 1914 by Roland Edgar Cooper who became Curator of the Botanic Garden in 1934. The cross was made by Charles Lamont, an assistant curator at the Garden. He had hoped to produce a plant which had the best characteristics of its parents but he was so disappointed with the results that he threw them on the compost heap. Later, the cross was repeated by Charles Puddle at Bodnant Gardens, Wales with more success. The first cultivar to be named was 'Dawn' followed by 'Deben'. After he died another cultivar was named 'Charles Lamont' in his honour.

V. × *bodnantense* was described by William Thomas Stearn, who had a distinguished career in botanical science. Stearn worked as Librarian for the Royal Horticultural Society and later as a scientific officer in the Botany Department of the British Museum (Natural History), London. He was also a visiting professor at the University of Cambridge and President of the Linnaean Society. *V.* × *bodnantense* was also described by Henry Duncan McLaren, Lord Aberconway, who inherited Bodnant Garden.

Bodnant Garden was developed by Henry and Agnes Pochin. Henry Davis Pochin was an industrialist who moved to Bodnant Hall with his wife on retirement in 1874. He employed Edward Milner, a landscape designer, to develop the shrubberies into a garden where specimen plants from around the world could be displayed. When Henry died in 1895 his estate was inherited by his daughter Laura Elizabeth Pochin, who was also a garden enthusiast. In 1877 she had married Charles McLaren and he took over the running of the many companies that Laura's father owned. McLaren was made a peer in 1911 and became the first Lord Aberconway. In 1901 Charles and Laura's son Henry, on leaving the University of Cambridge, took over the running of the garden. He was just twenty-one years old and a garden enthusiast like his mother. He sponsored plant-hunting expeditions, and plant hunters such as George Forrest, Ernest Wilson and Frank Kingdon-Ward brought back plants to Bodnant. Charles Puddle became Head Gardener at Bodnant in 1947, following in the footsteps of his father Frederick, who had been appointed Head Gardener in 1920.

The cultivar *V.* × *bodnantense* 'Dawn' is an ornamental, upright, deciduous shrub. It is a popular cultivar with fragrant light-pink and white clusters of tubular flowers, which appear from red buds on bare branches from autumn to spring. Insects pollinate the flowers. The leaves, which are ovate and toothed, are bronze-coloured when they emerge but gradually turn to dark green. They become a vibrant copper colour before they fall. The flowers are followed by single-seeded fruit, which turn from red to an attractive blue-black as they mature. The plant has received the Royal Horticultural Society's Award of Garden Merit.

Viburnum × *bodnantense* 'Dawn'
Artist: Linda Ambler
Graphite pencil, watercolour and coloured pencil
Accepted to the Archive 2006

Viburnum opulus L.
Viburnum opulus 'Xanthocarpum'

Family: Viburnaceae

Viburnum opulus, commonly known as the guelder rose, is in the family Viburnaceae. Its native range is from Europe to Siberia and Turkey. *V. opulus* is naturalized from Canada to the northern states of the US and known there as the cranberry bush. The plant does well on moist alkaline soils and can be found in woods, scrub and hedgerows.

One of the earliest drawings of *V. opulus* is by Leonardo da Vinci, dated between 1506 and 1512. The drawing is executed in red and white chalk on orange-red paper. Da Vinci thought the plant he drew was an acer or maple, but it has since been identified as *V. opulus*. The drawing shows a cluster of berries and some leaves; it was originally bequeathed to Francesco Melzi, one of da Vinci's pupils. The drawing was added to the Royal Collection around 1690.

V. opulus is a hardy, ornamental, deciduous shrub with grey stems. It is a useful addition to a garden shrubbery as it is an important plant for wildlife. The flowers are rich in nectar and pollen which are attractive to bees and other insects, such as hoverflies, and it is an important plant for butterflies, moths and some caterpillars. *V. opulus* has opposite, three-lobed, green leaves with serrated edges. An identification feature is the location of hairs on the underside of the leaves situated where the lateral veins join the mid-rib. The leaf petioles have a channel with stipules above the leaf base and rounded glands near the apex. The leaves turn an eye-catching red-purple in the autumn. The white flowers are terminal and hermaphrodite; they have pedicels of varying length so that the whole flower appears as a flat-headed umbel. The large, showy, white outer florets are sterile and have large white petals. These larger flowers surround a cluster of smaller, inner, fertile flowers with reduced petals and yellow anthers. The stigma is three-lobed. The red fruits are translucent red drupes, each containing a single seed. Many garden birds, including bullfinches and mistle thrushes, eat the fruits and help disperse the seeds. *V. opulus* frequently forms adventitious roots and new vertical shoots on branches which touch the ground.

The cultivar *V. opulus* 'Xanthocarpum' has been given the Royal Horticultural Society's Award of Garden Merit. It is noted for its golden-yellow translucent fruits and glossy, apple-green leaves which turn yellow in autumn.

V. opulus was developed by Späth's nursery in Berlin around 1910. The nursery was created in 1720 by Christoph Späth and in 1863 it was moved to south-east Berlin. In 1879 an arboretum was developed by Franz Ludwig Späth; his son, Hellmut Ludwig Späth, took over the garden after his father's death. After Hellmut's death the garden passed into public ownership. Since 1961 it has been part of the teaching and research programme of Humboldt University. *V. opulus* 'Xanthocarpum' received a First-Class Certificate in 1966, when it was shown by the Crown Estate Commissioners at the Royal Windsor Rose and Horticultural Society Show.

Viburnum opulus
Artist: Cathrine Allsopp
Graphite pencil and watercolour
Accepted to the Archive 2008

Viburnum opulus 'Xanthocarpum'
Artist: Barbara Munro
Watercolour and pen and ink
Accepted to the Archive 2011

Weigela 'Gold Rush'
Weigela 'Briant Rubidor' = 'Olympiade'
Weigela florida 'Alexandra'

Family: Caprifoliaceae

Sheffield Botanical Gardens hold the national collections of *Weigela* and *Diervilla*. The two genera are very close. *Weigela* is native to north China, Korea and Japan whereas *Diervilla*'s native range is eastern North America.

Weigela is a deciduous shrub in the honeysuckle family, Caprifoliaceae. In 1929 *Weigela* and *Diervilla* were separated by Liberty Hyde Bailey, an American horticulturalist, botanist and taxonomist. One of the differences between *Weigela* and *Diervilla* is that the flowers on the latter develop at the end of the current season's growth, whereas in the former the flowers appear along the flowering stem in its second year. *Diervilla* flowers have five lobes forming a two-lipped corolla joined at the base to form a tube. *Weigela* flowers are funnel-shaped, usually with five equal lobes. Both genera have simple opposite leaves with serrated edges. Some *Weigela* fruits have winged seeds.

Weigela is named after Christian Ehrenfried von Weigel, a Swedish physician, chemist and botanist, who studied at the University of Greifswald and at the University of Göttingen. In 1772 he became Supervisor of the Botanical Garden at the University of Greifswald. In 1842, after the Treaty of Nanking at the end of the First Opium War, the Royal Horticultural Society decided to send a plant collector to China. The person they chose to collect for them was Robert Fortune. He was given a list of 'collecting' instructions by the Royal Horticultural Society's 'China Committee' which included a request to collect hardy plants that would grow in British gardens. He was to report to the Committee on a regular basis and keep detailed notes. Fortune travelled first to Hong Kong on board HMS *Emu* which left Britain in 1843. After plant collecting in the hills around Hong Kong, he sailed to Amoy and then to the island of Chusan. Fortune discovered *W. florida* in 1844 growing in the 'Grotto Garden' owned by a mandarin in Chusan. He described the plant as full of rose-coloured flowers, hanging in graceful bunches from the axils of the leaves and ends of the branches. Fortune noted that the gardens of the mandarins were so small that only plants of special merit were grown there. He introduced the plant to Britain in 1845.

The species *W. florida* was described by Alexander Georg von Bunge (1803–90). Bunge was a Russian-German physician who was also a professor of botany. In 1830–31 he travelled to China on a scientific expedition. When the plant arrived in England, it was planted in a greenhouse in the Royal Horticultural Society's garden at Chiswick. It was soon discovered to be hardy and became a popular garden shrub. It was exhibited at the Regent's Park Show where Queen Victoria showed interest in it, prompting the Duke of Norfolk to present her with a specimen. The three hybrids illustrated are in the National Collection at Sheffield Botanical Gardens.

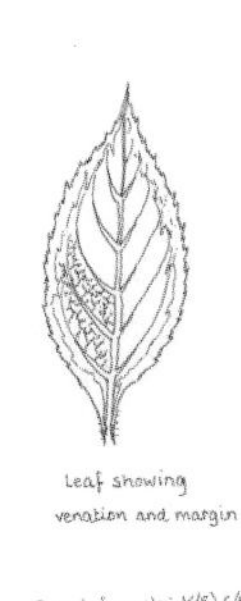

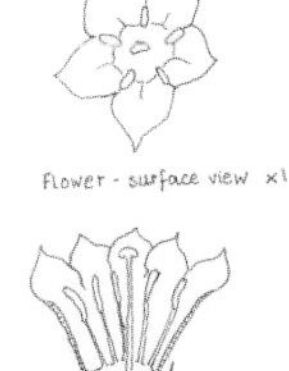

W. 'Gold Rush'
Artist: Barbara Munro
Watercolour and pen and ink
Accepted to the Archive 2012

W. 'Briant Rubidor' = 'Olympiade'
Artist: Judyth Pickles
Graphite pencil and watercolour
Accepted to the Archive 2011

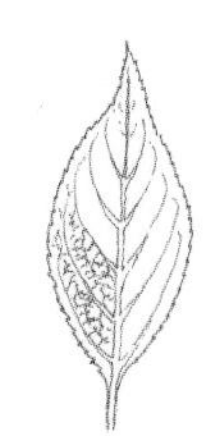

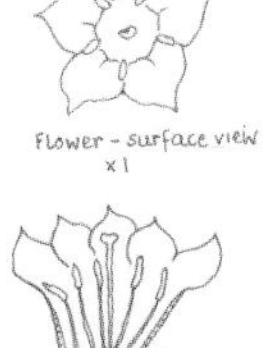

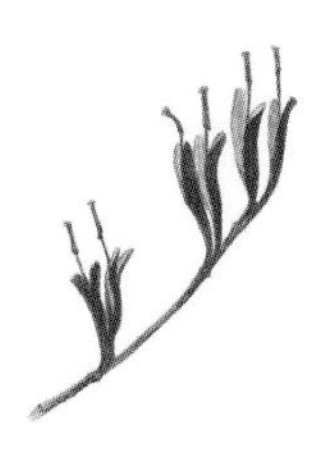

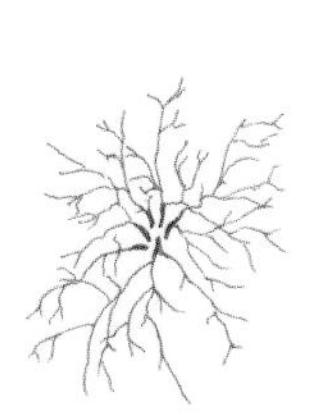

W. florida 'Alexandra'
Artist: Barbara Munro
Watercolour and pen and ink
Accepted to the Archive 2012

Geranium pratense L.
Centaurea scabiosa L.
Leucanthemum vulgare Lam.
Knautia arvensis (L.) Coult.

In 2005 Florilegium Society member Margaret Sanderson offered the Society a set of Royal Horticultural Society award-winning illustrations of wildflowers. The Florilegium Society selection panel accepted the illustrations which related to plants growing in the Dark and White Peak districts of Derbyshire. In 2004 the Gardens had sourced and planted a number of local Peak District plants in order to create a new wildflower area. Sadly, the plants did not survive. It appears that in a botanical garden it is virtually impossible to recreate the ideal growing conditions for individual plants that are found in the wild. The geographical location, the weather, soil type and hybridization all need careful monitoring. There is also the danger of cross-pollination from any nearby wild populations. Competition or lack of it could alter the general appearance of the plant, particularly its size. These considerations become concerns for conservation if the plants are to be reintroduced to boost the wild population.

A supporter of the Sheffield planting and of The Florilegium Society was Michael Hickey, a horticulturalist and botanical artist. He intended to visit the Botanical Gardens to see the native plants but illness prevented him from making the journey to Yorkshire. In 2005 he was awarded a posthumous M.Phil. degree from the University of Reading for a thesis entitled 'Habit Creation in Botanical Gardens'.

Geranium pratense or meadow cranesbill is a member of the Geraniaceae family. It was first described by Linnaeus and has green, rounded, palmately divided leaves. The dish-shaped flowers have five blue-violet petals. It is an attractive plant of waysides and traditional hay-meadows.

Centaurea scabiosa or greater knapweed is a perennial and member of the Asteraceae family; it was first described by Linnaeus. *C. scabiosa* grows in limestone areas and thrives in poor soil. It has dark green, deeply dissected leaves and purple flowers. It is distinguished from *C. nigra*, common knapweed, by an outer ring of ray florets. It has a range of insect pollinators including bees and butterflies.

Leucanthemum vulgare or ox-eye daisy is an herbaceous perennial and member of the Asteraceae family. It was first described by Jean Baptiste Pierre Antoine de Monet Lamarck, a French biologist and a forerunner of the theory of evolution, who worked as a botanist at the Jardin des Plantes in Paris. *L. vulgare* has a disc of yellow florets surrounded by a ring of white ray florets. It has simple, toothed, spoon-shaped green leaves and can be found in swathes along waysides and in traditional hay-meadows.

Knautia arvensis or field scabious is a member of the Dipsacaceae family. It was first described by Linnaeus and also by Thomas Coulter, who was born in Ireland and studied medicine in Dublin. Coulter later worked at the Jardin des Plantes in Paris. He collected plants in California and Mexico whilst he was working for a silver-mining company. *K. arvensis* is a perennial with lilac-blue flowers and pink anthers. It is a plant of limestone meadows and attracts a wide range of pollinators including bees, butterflies and moths.

Top left: *Geranium pratense*
Top right: *Knautia arvensis*
Bottom left: *Leucanthemum vulgare*
Bottom right: *Centaurea scabiosa*
Artist: Margaret Sanderson
Graphite pencil and watercolour
Accepted to the Archive 2005

Xanthorrhoea australis R. Br.

Family: Asphodelaceae

Xanthorrhoea australis, the grass tree, is native to Australia and was described by the botanist Robert Brown in his *Prodromus Florae Novae Hollandiae et Insulae Van-Diemen* which appeared in 1810.

Brown studied medicine at the University of Edinburgh but did not take his degree. He was very interested in natural history and was keen to travel and pursue his studies. He joined the Fifeshire Regiment of Fencibles (home defence volunteers) as the surgeon's mate. When he was in London recruiting for the regiment, he met Joseph Banks's librarian, Jonas Dryander, and through him became a member of the Linnaean Society. As a recognized botanist he was able to study plants that Joseph Banks had previously brought back from Australia. In 1800 Banks wrote to Brown asking him if he would serve as naturalist on a trip to survey New Holland (Australia). In July 1801 he set sail on board HMS *Investigator* with Captain Matthew Flinders. The botanical artist Ferdinand Bauer was also on board. They arrived in Australia in December 1801. Eventually the *Investigator* became unfit for travel and Flinders had to return home to fetch another ship, but Brown and Bauer remained to continue their work in New South Wales, Tasmania and Norfolk Island. It was in these areas that they found *X. australis*. Brown described the plant after their return to England. The genus name *Xanthorrhoea* is taken from the Greek *xanthos* which means yellow and *rheo* meaning flow. This refers to the resinous gum which is found at the base of old leaves and used to make varnish, lacquer and adhesive.

X. australis is a perennial plant which develops a sturdy black trunk from which long, narrow, stiff, blue-green leaves appear, clustered at the top. The leaves are used in the floristry industry. The plant is very slow-growing. The trunk, which is sometimes branched, is made up from the layering of leaves and can take several years to form. The old leaves fall downwards to form a protective covering around the plant like a skirt which gives the plant some protection from fires. The flowers form a double spiral around a spike which grows very quickly up to 2 metres in height. The flowering spike is brown until the flowers open, then the colour changes to cream or white; the lower part of the spike does not have any flowers. Young plants mature and flower after about seven years, often stimulated by exposure to fire. The individual stemless flowers are scented and attract bees and nectar-loving birds. The fruit is a capsule, which contains a few black seeds which are dispersed when the capsule dries and opens. *X. australis* is long-lived. The plant is distinctive in the wild and is grown for interest in botanical gardens. It is growing in the pavilions at Sheffield Botanical Gardens.

Xanthorrhoea australis
Artist: Cathrine Allsopp
Coloured pencil
Accepted to the Archive 2006

♂
×3

Biographies of the artists

MARY ACTON was a primary school teacher until retirement. She was the Chairman and later President of the Northern Society for Botanical Art, founded in Sheffield in 1993. Mary completed the Certificate in Botanical Illustration at The University of Sheffield in 1997 and became a Founder Member and Fellow of the Sheffield Florilegium Society.

CATHRINE ALLSOPP attended art school in Cape Town. She studied botanical illustration at The University of Sheffield and became a Founder Member and Fellow of the Sheffield Florilegium Society. In 2018 Cathrine's illustration of *Xanthorrhoea australis* was chosen to illustrate the plant on a storyboard at Meise Botanic Garden, Belgium.

LINDA AMBLER has a degree in history from Durham University and worked as a history and primary teacher. She is a largely self-taught artist and enjoys attending regular classes in botanical art. In 2003 Linda went to Sri Lanka to paint the local flora with a group tutored by Valerie Oxley and organized by Higham Hall College, Cumbria.

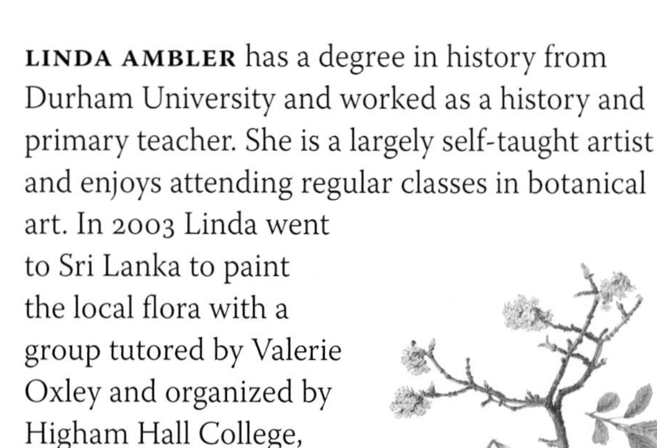

LESLEY BADGER is a Founder Member and Fellow of the Sheffield Florilegium Society. She has a degree in botany from The University of Sheffield and additional qualifications in education. Lesley worked as a lecturer in higher and further education and as a botany lecturer on the Diploma in Botanical Illustration course at The University of Sheffield.

ARNOLDA BEYNON currently lives in Australia but was resident in Sheffield when she studied for the Certificate in Botanical Illustration at The University of Sheffield. Arnolda is a Founder Member of the Sheffield Florilegium Society.

SUSAN CHRISTOPHER-COULSON worked in London as a fashion designer and illustrator following her B.A. degree. She has received two Gold Medals from the Royal Horticultural Society for her coloured pencil illustrations: 'A Garden Diary' in 1999 and 'Alpine Primula Auriculas' in 2001. Susan's work can be found in the RHS Lindley Library collections and the Shirley Sherwood Collection at Kew. She is a Founder Member of the Sheffield Florilegium Society.

ANNE DENT is a Founder Member and Fellow of the Sheffield Florilegium Society. She has a degree in horticulture from the University of Nottingham (Sutton Bonington) and a certificate in education from the University of Birmingham. Anne has exhibited at the Royal Horticultural Society and has a number of illustrations in the book *The Golden Age of Quaker Botanists*.

JO EDWARDS is a Founder Member and Fellow of the Sheffield Florilegium Society. She studied in Birmingham for a diploma in art and design and worked as a textile designer, art teacher and botanical illustrator. Jo was awarded the Diploma in Botanical Illustration from The University of Sheffield and is a member of the Chelsea Physic Garden Florilegium Society.

HELEN FITZGERALD was born in Sydney. She has a degree in art education and applied science and over fifty years' teaching experience. Helen was awarded the Royal Horticultural Society's Gold Medal for her botanical paintings of eucalypti in 2002. She is also a member of The Florilegium Society at the Royal Botanic Gardens Sydney, and has illustrated a number of books.

PAMELA FURNISS was a Founder Member and Fellow of the Sheffield Florilegium Society. In 2002 Pamela was awarded a Royal Horticultural Society Silver Medal for an exhibit of 'Hostas through the Seasons' in watercolour and pencil. She was invited to exhibit at the Society of Botanical Artists' exhibition in London in 2003.

JENNY HARRIS studied dentistry at Guy's Hospital, University of London and gained specialist qualifications in paediatric dentistry from the Royal College of Surgeons of England. She attends weekend and day-school courses in botanical illustration whenever time allows. Jenny is a Founder Member of the Sheffield Florilegium Society.

PATSY HIRST is a Founder Member of the Sheffield Florilegium Society and has been a lifelong passionate gardener and is a knowledgeable plantswoman. She was awarded the Certificate in Botanical Illustration from The University of Sheffield and was a member of a group of botanical artists who were awarded a Silver Gilt Medal by the Royal Horticultural Society for an exhibit called 'Watercolour Paintings of Plants from Sheffield Botanical Gardens.

JILL HOLCOMBE has an honours degree in botany from The University of Sheffield, also a diploma in education and a Certificate in Botanical Illustration. She has two RHS Silver-Gilt Group Awards and her work was included in the Sheffield Millennium Gallery's 'Can Art Save Us?' exhibition. Jill is a Founder Member and Fellow of the Sheffield Florilegium Society.

CAROLINE HOLLEY lives in Wales. She has a degree in geography and botany from the University of Newcastle and a City & Guilds teaching qualification. She has received two Gold Medals and a Silver Gilt Medal from the Royal Horticultural Society for her illustrations. Caroline has work in the RHS Lindley Library collections and the Hunt Institute for Botanical Documentation in the US.

JANE HOWELL trained as a dental nurse at Bristol Dental Hospital. She has exhibited at the Royal Horticultural Society, receiving a Silver Medal in 2004 and a Silver Gilt Medal the following year. Jane exhibited 'Clematis in Watercolour' at the Royal Caledonian Horticultural Society Show in 2006 and received a Silver Medal. She is a Founder Member and Fellow of the Sheffield Florilegium Society.

JUNE MARY HUCKERBY followed a career in nursing. She was awarded the Diploma in Botanical Illustration from The University of Sheffield in 2000. June undertook a teaching course at Rother Valley College, Dinnington and has since organized a number of classes in botanical illustration, some of her students subsequently joining The Florilegium Society.

JENNY KIRKLAND was awarded the Certificate in Botanical Illustration from The University of Sheffield and became a Founder Member of the Florilegium Society. She designed the Society's logo and has continued to combine her interest in botanical illustration with the mediums of stained glass and ceramics since moving to Cheshire in 2015.

The Florilegium Society

LOUISE LANE studied in Leeds for a degree in graphic design and illustration and was awarded a post-graduate certificate in education from The University of Sheffield. She has been awarded three Gold Medals from the Royal Horticultural Society and has work in the RHS Lindley Library collections. Louise exhibited at the Hunt Institute for Botanical Documentation in 2019.

JULIE MASON received a diploma in painting and drawing from the London Art College and later she was awarded the Society of Botanical Artists' Distance Learning Diploma. In 2013 she became the first Keeper of the Sheffield Florilegium Society's Herbarium. Julie became a Fellow of the Sheffield Florilegium Society in 2016.

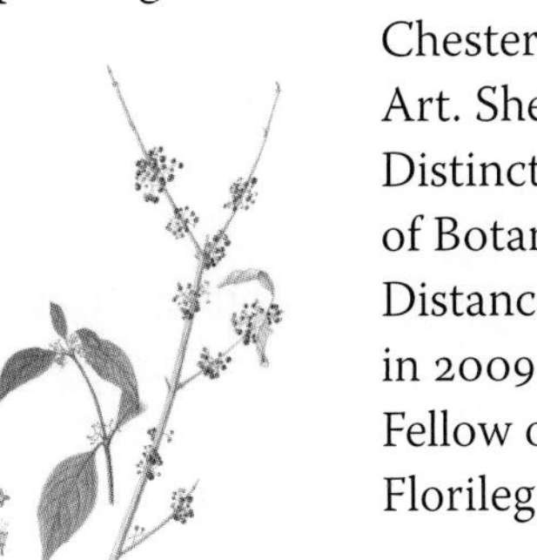

ELENI MCLOUGHLIN was born in Cyprus. She was awarded the Certificate in Botanical Illustration from the University of Birmingham. Eleni has been awarded medals for her illustrations in England and Scotland. Her illustrations of rare and endangered plants are published in the *Red Data Book of the Flora of Cyprus*. Eleni is the Archive Organizer for the Sheffield Florilegium Society.

NEELAM MODI is an Indian-born illustrator who uses several styles and media. She loves the freedom and fun of children's illustration and the discipline and precision of botanical illustration. Neelam became a Fellow of the Sheffield Florilegium Society in 2012 and she is also a Fellow of the Chelsea Physic Garden Florilegium Society.

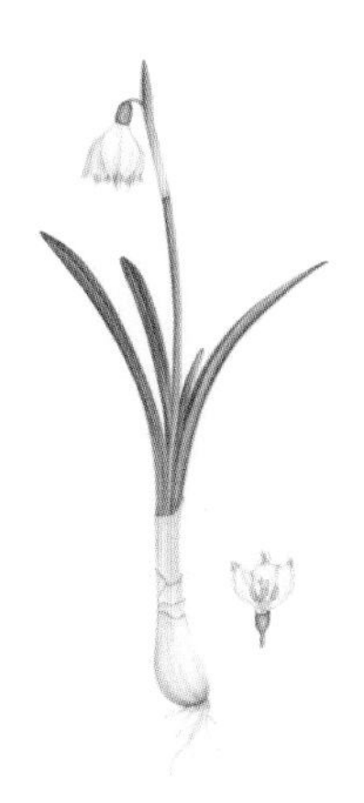

MARY MORTON attended Chesterfield College of Art. She was awarded a Distinction in the Society of Botanical Artists' Distance Learning Diploma in 2009 and became a Fellow of the Sheffield Florilegium Society in 2019.

BARBARA MUNRO has an honours degree in botany from Durham University and a certificate in ecology and conservation from Birkbeck, University of London. Barbara was awarded a Distinction on completion of the Society of Botanical Artists' Distance Learning Programme and is a Fellow of the Society of Botanical Artists and the Sheffield Florilegium Society.

SUE NICHOLLS has a degree in biological sciences from Aston University, Birmingham and worked as a medical librarian at The University of Sheffield. She completed the Certificate in Botanical Illustration from The University of Sheffield in 2000 and was awarded an RHS Silver Gilt Medal for studies of the Ericaceae family in 2002. Sue is a Founder Member and Fellow of the Sheffield Florilegium Society.

VALERIE OXLEY has a certificate in education from Hereford College of Education. In 1995 she worked with Dr Patrick Harding to develop the Diploma in Botanical Illustration at The University of Sheffield. Valerie wrote the book *Botanical Illustration* published by The Crowood Press in 2008. She is an Honorary Retired Member of the Society of Botanical Artists and President of the Institute for Analytical Plant Illustration. Valerie is the Founding Chairman and a Fellow of the Sheffield Florilegium Society.

JUDYTH PICKLES has a diploma in fine art from the Ruskin School of Art at the University of Oxford. She has exhibited at the Royal Horticultural Society and received medals for exhibits of Liliaceae in 1994 and Pleione in 2003. Judyth's work appears in *The Wild Flowers of the Peak District* by Patrick Harding and Valerie Oxley.

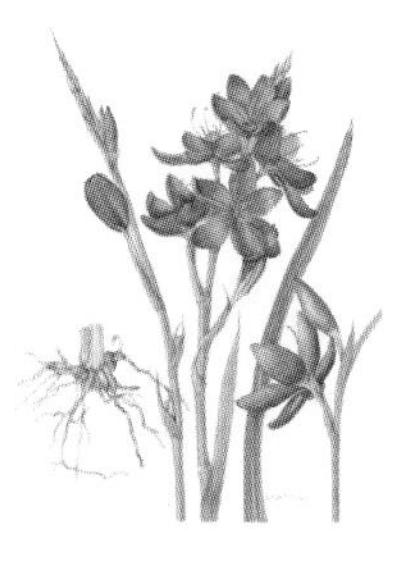

JANICE RELTON has a national diploma in dairying and a certificate in laboratory management. Janice was a laboratory technician in the Genetics Department at The University of Sheffield and in retirement took up botanical illustration. She was awarded the Certificate in Botanical Illustration from The University of Sheffield in 1997. Janice is a Founder Member of the Sheffield Florilegium Society.

MARGARET SANDERSON trained as a nurse. In 1999 she was awarded a Royal Horticultural Society Medal for watercolour paintings of 'Nectar Plants, Seeds and Fruit'. In 2002 she was awarded an RHS Silver Medal for paintings of 'Colourful Climbers'. She became a Fellow of the Sheffield Florilegium Society in 2005.

ELAINE SHIMWELL worked as a secretary in administration. She completed the Certificate in Botanical Illustration at The University of Sheffield in 2002 and in 2004 she was awarded a Silver Gilt Medal by the Royal Horticultural Society for drawings of wild flowers in graphite. Elaine is a Founder Member and Fellow of the Sheffield Florilegium Society.

JULIE SMALL followed a career in teaching. In 2000 she received a Gold Medal from the Royal Horticultural Society for a series of graphite drawings. Her work is held in the Shirley Sherwood Collection, the RHS Lindley Library collections, the National Museum of Wales, Cardiff and the Hunt Institute for Botanical Documentation. Julie's drawings have been shown in several books on botanical art.

SHEILA STANCILL studied at Guildford School of Art and Bath Academy of Art at Corsham Court. She lives in Sheffield and has a degree in science from the Open University and the Certificate in Botanical Illustration from The University of Sheffield. Sheila has exhibited three times at the Royal Horticultural Society and is a Founder Member and Fellow of the Sheffield Florilegium Society.

SALLY STRAWSON attended art school and afterwards became an interior designer. She has work in the Hunt Institute for Botanical Documentation and was invited to contribute to the *Highgrove Florilegium* and the *Transylvania Florilegium*. Sally is a Fellow of the Sheffield Florilegium Society and a member of The Florilegium Society at the Royal Botanic Gardens Sydney.

VIVIENNE TAYLOR was awarded the Diploma of Botanical Illustration from The University of Sheffield. She is a Founder Member and Fellow of the Sheffield Florilegium Society. Vivienne is also a Fellow of the Chelsea Physic Garden Florilegium Society and Fellow of the Society of Botanical Artists.

ROSALIND TIMPERLEY has a teaching certificate from Goldsmiths, University of London and became a primary teacher. She was awarded the Certificate in Botanical Illustration from The University of Sheffield and received the Royal Horticultural Society's Lindley Silver Medal for paintings of English apples in 2012. Rosalind was elected Chair of The Florilegium Society at Sheffield Botanical Gardens in 2015.

Acknowledgements and information sources

Just when you've learnt how to spell the name of a plant, they change it!
DR KEN THOMPSON

Thank you to Jill Holcombe, Secretary of the Florilegium Society and to Susan Turner of the Friends of the Botanical Gardens (FOBS) for reading through the text and for their continued support and encouragement. Thank you to Ian Turner, Curator of the Sheffield Botanical Gardens, for his help with naming plants, and to Lukman Sinclair for all his care and expertise in copying the images. Last but not least, thank you to the contributing artists for their valuable comments about the plants they have illustrated.

Information about Plants

Camellias: Stephen Lyus, Rhododendron, Camellia & Magnolia Group and International Camellia Society.

Castanea sativa: Dr Rob Jarman, Research Associate, University of Gloucestershire.

Clivia miniata: Graham D. Duncan, Botanist and Specialist Bulb Horticulturalist, Kirstenbosch National Botanical Garden, South Africa.

Galanthus nivalis: Cambridge University Botanic Garden, at www.botanic.cam.ac.uk

Hedychium gardnerianum: Dr Mark Watson, Head of Major Floras, Royal Botanic Garden, Edinburgh.

Hesperantha coccinea: Dr Ken Thompson, Retired Senior Lecturer, The University of Sheffield.

Hydrangea macrophylla: Judith Johnson, Hydrangea Collection Curator, Holehird Gardens, Cumbria.

Primula vulgaris: Philip Gilmartin, Professor of Plant Molecular Genetics, University of Hull.

Prunus serrula: Robert Vernon (sen.), Bluebell Arboretum & Nursery, near Ashby-de-la-Zouch, Leicestershire.

Sarcococca confusa: Alastair Culham, Associate Professor of Botany, School of Biological Sciences, and Curator, University of Reading Herbarium.

Stachyurus praecox: Dr Stephen A. Harris, Druce Curator of Oxford University Herbaria.

Viburnum × bodnantense 'Dawn': Dr Alan Elliott, Biodiversity Network Manager for World Flora Online, Royal Botanic Garden, Edinburgh.

Lindsay Durrant, RHS Plant Finder Compiler, Horticultural Advice and Information, RHS Wisley.

Dr Kanchi N. Gandhi, Senior Nomenclature Registrar, Harvard University Herbaria, Cambridge, Massachusetts, for information on plant names and families.

International Plant Names Index (IPNI), organized collaboratively by the Royal Botanic Gardens, Kew, Harvard University Herbaria & Libraries and Australian National Botanic Gardens, at www.ipni.org

Plants of the World Online (POWO), facilitated by the Royal Botanic Gardens, Kew, at www.plantsoftheworldonline.org

National Collections of Sarcococca, Diervilla and Weigela, Friends of Sheffield Botanical Gardens, at www.fobssheffield.co.uk

Trees and Shrubs Online, at www.treesandshrubsonline.org

Bibliography

Arnold, Marion, *South African Botanical Art: Peeling Back the Petals* (Fernwood Press, 2001)

Bean, W.J., *Trees and Shrubs Hardy in the British Isles*, vols 1–4 (John Murray, revised 1973–80)

Bishop, Matt, Davis, Aaron, and Grimshaw, John, *A Monograph of Cultivated Galanthus* (Griffin Press, 2001)

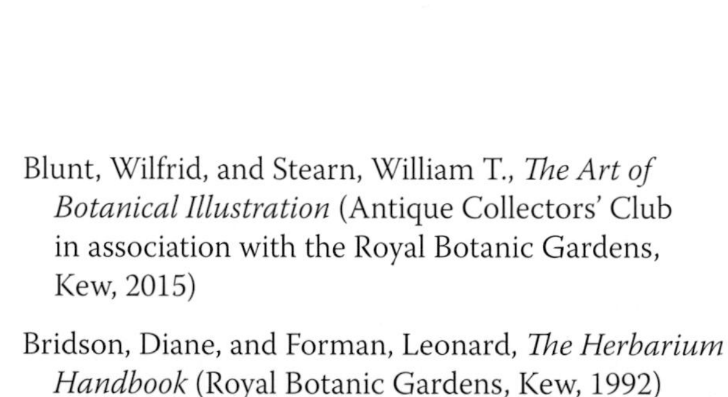

Paeonia ludlowii Jill Holcombe. Graphite pencil and watercolour. Accepted to the Archive 2006

Blunt, Wilfrid, and Stearn, William T., *The Art of Botanical Illustration* (Antique Collectors' Club in association with the Royal Botanic Gardens, Kew, 2015)

Bridson, Diane, and Forman, Leonard, *The Herbarium Handbook* (Royal Botanic Gardens, Kew, 1992)

Brown, Andrew, *Flower Paintings from the Apothecaries' Garden* (Antique Collectors' Club, 2005)

Brown, Andrew, *Botanical Illustration from Chelsea Physic Garden* (Antique Collectors' Club 2015)

Campbell-Culver, Maggie, *The Origin of Plants* (Headline, 2001)

Cox, Kenneth (ed.), *Frank Kingdon Ward's Riddle of the Tsangpo Gorges* (Garden Art Press, 2008)

Crane, Peter, *Ginkgo* (Yale University Press, 2013)

Davis, Aaron P., *The Genus Galanthus* (Royal Botanic Gardens, Kew in association with Timber Press, 1999)

Desmond, Ray, *Sir Joseph Dalton Hooker, Traveller and Plant Collector* (Antique Collectors' Club with the Royal Botanic Gardens, Kew, 1999)

Fish, Lyn, *Preparing Herbarium Specimens* (National Botanical Institute, Pretoria, South Africa, 1999)

Flanagan, Mark, and Kirkham, Tony, *Wilson's China: A Century On* (Kew Publishing, 2009)

Franklin, Ros, *A Coming of Age: Celebrating 18 Years of Botanical Painting by the Eden Project Florilegium Society* (Two Rivers Press, 2018)

Fraser, Michael (text), with McMahon, Liz (illustrations), *Between Two Shores: Flora and Fauna of the Cape of Good Hope* (David Phillip, 1994)

Grey-Wilson, Christopher, *The Genus Cyclamen* (Royal Botanic Gardens, Kew in association with Christopher Helm and Timber Press, 1988)

Grey-Wilson, Christopher, and Mathew, Brian, *Bulbs: The Bulbous Plants of Europe and Their Allies* (Collins, 1981)

Harris, Stephen, *The Magnificent Flora Graeca* (Bodleian Library, University of Oxford, 2007)

Harris, Stephen, *Planting Paradise: Cultivating the Garden 1501–1900* (Bodleian Library, University of Oxford, 2011)

Hemery, Gabriel, and Simblet, Sarah, *The New Sylva* (Bloomsbury, 2014)

Heywood, V.H., Brummitt, R.K., Culham, A., and Seberg, O., *Flowering Plant Families of the World* (Royal Botanic Gardens, Kew, 2007)

Huxley, Anthony, Griffiths, Mark, and Levy, Margot, *The New RHS Dictionary of Gardening*, 4 vols (Macmillan, reprinted 1997)

Kelly, John (ed.), *The Hillier Gardener's Guide to Trees and Shrubs* (David & Charles, 1995)

Lack, H. Walter, *A Garden for Eternity: The Codex Liechtenstein* (Benteli, Berne, 2000)

Lawson, Elizabeth, *Primrose* (Reaktion, 2019)

Lawson-Hall, Toni, and Rothera, Brian, *Hydrangeas: A Gardeners' Guide* (Batsford, 1999)

Cynara cardunculus Neelam Modi. Pen and ink. Accepted to the Archive 2014

Lindsay, Ann, *Seeds of Blood and Beauty: Scottish Plant Explorers* (Birlinn, 2005)

Lindsay Mitchell, Ann, and House, Syd, *David Douglas: Explorer and Botanist* (Aurum, 1999)

Mabberley, David J., *Mabberley's Plant Book* (Cambridge University Press, 2017)

McLean, Brenda, *A Pioneering Plantsman: A.K. Bulley and the Great Plant Hunters* (The Stationery Office, 1997)

McLean, Brenda, *George Forrest: Plant Hunter* (Antiques Collectors' Club in association with the Royal Botanic Garden, Edinburgh, 2004)

More, David, and White, John, *Cassell's Trees of Britain and Northern Europe* (Cassell, 2003)

Morris, Colleen, and Murray, Louisa, *The Florilegium: The Royal Botanic Gardens Sydney: Celebrating 200 years* (Kew Publishing, Royal Botanic Gardens, Kew, 2016)

Musgrave, Toby, Gardner, Chris, and Musgrave, Will, *The Plant Hunters* (Ward Lock, 1998)

Nichols, Ann, *The Golden Age of Quaker Botanists* (The Quaker Tapestry at Kendal, Cumbria, 2006)

Nikulinsky, Philippa, and Hopper, Stephen D., *Soul of the Desert* (Freemantle Arts Centre, 2007)

Oxley, Valerie, *Botanical Illustration* (The Crowood Press, 2008)

Phillips, Roger, and Rix, Martyn, *Perennials*, vols 1 and 2 (Macmillan, 1993 and 1996)

Phillips, Roger, and Rix, Martyn, *Conservatory and Indoor Plants*, vols 1 and 2 (Pan, 1998)

Phillips, Roger, and Rix, Martyn, *The Botanical Garden*, vols 1 and 2 (Macmillan, 2002)

Rice, Graham, and Strangman, Elizabeth, *The Gardener's Guide to Growing Hellebores* (David & Charles, 1993)

Richards, John (text), with Edwards, Brigid (illustrations), *Primula* (Batsford, 2002)

Shephard, Sue, *Seeds of Fortune: A Gardening Dynasty* (Bloomsbury, 2003)

Short, Philip, *In Pursuit of Plants* (Timber Press, 2004)

The scientific names of the plants appeared as accepted names in the 2020 RHS Plant Finder and IPNI (International Plant Name Index) and are correct at the time of going to press.